HERBAGE INTAKE
HANDBOOK

Edited by:
J.D. LEAVER

Published by:
The British Grassland Society

First published 1982
Reprinted 1985

ISBN 0 905944 06 2

The authors or their informants have had direct experience of the items of equipment and proprietary products identified by name. However, the comments made in this book are not intended to be exhaustive and no exclusive endorsement of named products is implied.

CONTENTS

LIST OF CONTRIBUTORS

R.D. BAKER, BSc, MSc, CDFM, Deputy Head of the Animal Nutrition and Production Division and Co-ordinator of grazing research, The Grassland Research Institute, Hurley, Maidenhead, Berks.

M. CHENOST, Ingénieur Agronome, Mâitre de Recherches à l'INRA, Laboratoire des Aliments, Centre de Recherches Zootechniques et Vétérinaires, Institut National de la Recherche Agronomique, Theix 63110 Beaumont, France.

C. DEMARQUILLY, Ingénieur Agronome, Directeur-Adjoint de Recherches à l'INRA, Directeur du Laboratoire des Aliments, Centre de Recherches Zootechniques et Vétérinaires, Institut National de la Recherche Agronomique, Theix 63110 Beaumont, France.

J.F.D. GREENHALGH, MA, MS, PhD, Professor of Animal Production and Health, Department of Agriculture, University of Aberdeen, Aberdeen.

J. HODGSON, BSc, PhD, Head of Grazing Ecology Department, Hill Farming Research Organisation, Bush Estate, Penicuik, Midlothian.

W. HOLMES, BSc, PhD, DSc, NDA, NDD, FIBiol, Professor of Agriculture, Wye College, University of London, Wye, Nr. Ashford, Kent.

A. KEEN, Ir, MSc, Member of the Wageningen Section, Institute TNO for Mathematics, Information Processing and Statistics, Staringgebouw, Marijkeweg 11, 6700 AB Wageningen, The Netherlands.

J.D. LEAVER, BSc, PhD, Farm Director, Crichton Royal Farm, The West of Scotland Agricultural College, Dumfries.

Y.L.P. LE DU, BSc, PhD, Member of the Animal Nutrition and Production Division, The Grassland Research Institute, Hurley, Maidenhead, Berks.

J.A.C. MEIJS, Dr, Ir, Member of the Department of Ruminants, Institute for Livestock Feeding and Nutrition, Runderweg 2, 8200 AD Lelystad, The Netherlands.

P.D. PENNING, MI Biol, Member of the Animal Nutrition and Production Division, The Grassland Research Institute, Hurley, Maidenhead, Berks.

R.J.K. WALTERS, BSc, Member of the Grassland Agronomy Department, Welsh Plant Breeding Station, Plas Gogerddan, Nr. Aberystwyth.

PREFACE

The production of this *Herbage Intake Handbook* was brought about following recommendations made by the European Grazing Workshop Group to the British Grassland Society.

In view of the economic importance of animal production from grazed herbage, the appearance of the Handbook is timely. It can be well argued that the small amount of research and development effort directed towards grazing studies compared with indoor controlled feeding studies, is disproportionate to the needs of the animal production industries. Measuring herbage intake involves laborious techniques which are more susceptible to bias and error than indoor controlled techniques. However, grazed grass as a cost to the farmer represents about half that of conserved grass per unit of metabolisable energy, and a quarter of the cost of purchased concentrate. Increasing the utilisation of grazed herbage is thus an important priority, and herbage intake is an essential measurement in many grazing experiments.

A number of publications of grassland research techniques are already available which include chapters or parts of chapters outlining techniques for measuring herbage intake, but this Handbook for the first time brings together under one cover an outline of the various techniques available. It is a companion to the *Sward Measurement Handbook* edited by J. Hodgson, R.D. Baker, Alison Davies, A.S. Laidlaw and J.D. Leaver also published by the British Grassland Society.

The objectives of the Handbook are to describe those methods of measuring herbage intake and ingestive behaviour considered to be of potential value, and to assess their relevance for particular experimental requirements. The authors are experts in their own fields who have been actively involved in herbage intake studies. The views expressed concerning the relative importance of different techniques are necessarily those of the authors, and it is not claimed that the reviews and descriptions of techniques are exhaustive. Also the use of commercial names applied to pieces of equipment does not imply that alternatives are unavailable.

I am extremely grateful to the authors of chapters and to Professor Holmes for writing the Foreword, for the time and effort they have put into communicating such a difficult subject area. I hope they will be rewarded by an upsurge of interest in grazing studies which will be of benefit to all.

I am particularly indebted to members of the working group who gave great assistance in helping to devise the initial layout of the handbook, and subsequently in refereeing chapters. The group included; Dr. J. Hodgson, Hill Farming Research Organisation; Dr. Y.L.P. Le Du, Grassland Research Institute; Dr. J.A.C. Meijs, Institute for Livestock Feeding and Nutrition Research, Lelystad; Mr. P.D. Penning, Grassland Research Institute; and Mr. R.J.K. Walters, Welsh Plant Breeding Station. Thanks are also due to Mr. N.E. Young who as Secretary of the British Grassland Society made the initial arrangements for the working group and organised the translation into English of Chapter 5.

Finally I would like to thank Mrs June McCallay for the many painstaking hours she put into typing and correcting drafts of chapters and preparing the final typescript.

May 1982   J.D. Leaver, *Dumfries*

FOREWORD

Grass and forage crops provide most of the total world feed resources for ruminant livestock. A large proportion of their produce is harvested by grazing livestock and much of the remainder, conserved for winter or the dry season, is fed under *ad libitum* conditions. Although the farmer or grazier can assess performance of his pastures from the sales of stock or their produce there is not only considerable intrinsic scientific interest but the possibility of a better understanding leading to better utilisation of grazing and forage, if the quantities of food which ruminants consume and the factors which influence these quantities are understood. This topic, the measurement of voluntary intake of freely feeding animals, has been the subject of much effort in the past 25 years.

The British Grassland Society as part of its recent policy to increase and disseminate knowledge of the production and utilisation of grassland has commissioned several publications. One of these is this herbage intake handbook prepared by a small group of experts on their respective subjects and co-ordinated and edited by Dr. Leaver. It is a particular pleasure to record that as a result of collaboration with the European Grazing Workshop, the authorship includes experts from France and the Netherlands as well as from the United Kingdom.

As an aside may I comment that it continues to fascinate me that we have now developed such precise methods of estimating the intake of grazing animals. Even the so called direct methods are an achievement and the indirect methods seem little short of miraculous.

The handbook gives an historical introduction to the subject of intake measurement, stresses the difficulty and expense of all such activities and poses searching questions on the objectives of the experimenter. Subsequent chapters then discuss in detail the range of techniques which have been developed; the indirect clipping methods, the faecal index methods, estimation from feeding standards, assessment of voluntary intake indoors and the recording of ingestive behaviour. The methodology and limitations of each of these are considered.

A particular problem with pastures and with farm livestock is the inherent biological variability. Herbage intake studies must be designed statistically so that real and important differences can be distinguished from random biological variation. The need for precision is now facilitated in some respects by automation although much of the work on intake measurements is still heavily demanding in labour and effort. These new and developing methods are included in the text.

The handbook therefore endeavours to cover all the major methods and techniques at present available, with particular reference to the more intensive lowland pastures. It should be of value to all interested in the subject of herbage intake measurement.

May 1982   W. Holmes, *Wye*

CHAPTER 1

AN INTRODUCTION TO HERBAGE INTAKE MEASUREMENTS

J.F.D. Greenhalgh

1.1 REASONS FOR MEASURING HERBAGE INTAKE

The earliest investigators of grazing animals were probably induced to measure intake simply out of scientific curiosity. They observed animals grazing and they wished to know how much herbage these animals consumed. Today, scientific curiosity alone is not enough to justify the use of expensive research techniques, and there are more practical reasons for measuring intake.

Consider as an example an experiment to compare two varieties of a grass species in terms of animal production. For this experiment, two pure swards will be established, animals will be grazed upon them, and the productivity of these animals — as meat, milk or wool — will be recorded. The experiment may show that sward A promotes the production of, say, 10% more milk per hectare than sward B. The experimenter may be satisfied with this conclusion and may then recommend farmers to use A in preference to B. A more thorough investigator, however, will begin to ask more questions. Why was animal production greater for A? Did A outyield B in herbage dry matter grown? If not, was herbage from A more digestible than that from B? Was intake per animal per day higher for the superior variety? How much of the herbage accumulated by each variety was actually consumed by the animals? These questions are asked, not out of mere scientific curiosity, but because the answers to them are expected to lead to further improvements in animal productivity. The experimenter may wish to use the information provided by his experiment to establish principles of grassland utilisation, because he believes that only by identifying principles can he make improvements in any logical way. For example, if in this and other experiments the sward giving the greater animal productivity is that providing the greater intake per animal, then high intake is identified as a desirable characteristic that may legitimately be included among the herbage plant breeder's objectives. Further studies may reveal that high intake is associated with some physical characteristic of the grass leaf, such as the force needed to fracture it, and the latter may be used by the breeder to screen the numerous small samples of herbage from which he makes his initial selections.

In this example, the measurement of herbage intake serves firstly as a means of explaining differences in animal performance between two cultivars, secondly as the basis for a hypothesis that attempts to provide a more general explanation for such differences between cultivars, and thirdly as an aid to the plant breeder in producing better cultivars. This sequence of investigation, hypothesis and invention is a familiar one in many branches of applied science, and has been used frequently to bring about improvements in agriculture. In the important area of animal production from pasture, however, the sequence has not generally been followed in the logical manner exemplified above, because no satisfactory measures have been available of some essential steps in the processes by which grass is turned into animal products.

The absence of satisfactory methods for measuring herbage intake and its digestion by the grazing animal has almost certainly distorted progress in grassland utilisation. Plant breeders, until comparatively recently, concentrated their efforts on improving such agronomic characters of pasture plants as yield, persistency and winter hardiness, which could all be measured objectively. The acceptability of these plants to grazing animals could be assessed only subjectively, in terms of apparent "palatability", and thus tended to be neglected by plant breeders (although digestibility is recognised as an important trait). Herbage production has been steadily improved by the introduction of new varieties, and more dramatically by use of fertilizers, but there is little evidence of improvement in nutritive value. In six experiments in which the Aberystwyth strains of grasses were compared with their unimproved ancestors, the yield of herbage was often greater for the former, but there was no difference in that crude yet important measure of nutritive value, production per animal per unit time (Greenhalgh, 1969).

The example introducing this chapter featured a fairly simple experiment, but one in which plant breeder, agronomist, animal husbandman and nutritionist might all work together. In practice, such ideal collaboration is uncommon in experiments involving measurement of herbage intake. At one end of the spectrum, the plant breeder and agronomist may study intake in terms of the proportion of the herbage accumulated (by swards or single plants) that is consumed by grazing animals. At the other extreme, animal scientists may study the influence of concentrate supplements on the herbage intake of grazing animals. But in general, there is a need for more experiments involving all the disciplines.

1.2 PRINCIPLES OF THE METHODS USED TO MEASURE INTAKE

A primary division of the methods used to measure herbage intake is between those that estimate the loss from the pasture and those that estimate the gain to the animal. Historically, those of the first kind were originally used — as might be expected — by agronomists interested in extending their measures of herbage growth to include measures of herbage consumed, but they have also been used by nutritionists. Loss from the pasture is generally estimated by the difference $Y_1 - Y_2$, where Y_1 = herbage DM yield per unit area before grazing and Y_2 = yield after grazing. Allowance may also be made for the continuance of growth in the sward during the period of grazing. For example, a further series of yield estimates (Y_3) might be made simultaneously with Y_2, but in areas protected from grazing. If the grazed area is assumed to have achieved half the growth increment, $Y_3 - Y_1$, then herbage removed by grazing is calculated as $Y_1 + 0.5 (Y_3 - Y_1) - Y_2$, which simplifies to $0.5 (Y_1 + Y_3) - Y_2$. The complications of this approach, together with the techniques used to measure yield, are discussed in Chapter 2. To the nutritionist, two major disadvantages of sward loss methods are that they provide estimates only of gross intake of dry matter or its constituents, and that unless animals are grazed in individual enclosures (MacLusky, 1955) they do not give estimates of the intake of individual animals.

The simplest method of estimating intake as the herbage gained by the animal was that of Erizian (1932) who weighed animals before and after grazing. Although he corrected his estimates of intake for water consumed, urine and faeces excreted, and "insensible" (respiratory) losses, his method could not be described as accurate, and his estimates were in the form of total (wet) herbage consumed.

Most of the recently used methods of measuring intake have been based on one basically simple precept, that if the quantity (F kg) of dry matter (or of any nutrient) excreted in the faeces of a grazing animal can be measured, and if the digestibility (D, as a decimal) of the food dry matter (or nutrient) is known, then intake (I kg) can be calculated from the equation:

$$I = F/1-D \qquad\qquad (1.1)$$

This method was first described by Garrigus (1934), although according to Watson (1948) it had been used as early as 1928 at Imperial Chemical Industries' Jealott's Hill Research Station; later it was used and improved by Woodman *et al* (1937). The faeces output of grazing animals was measured by fitting them with collection bags, and digestibility by cutting herbage supposedly similar to that being grazed and giving it to other animals in a conventional balance trial. Although this technique represented a significant advance in methodology, it was soon criticised on the grounds of being cumbersome to both the animal (whose behaviour and intake might be affected by its burden of harness, bag and excreta) and to the experimenter (who, in addition to periodically relieving animals of their load of faeces, had also to cut and collect herbage for the balance trial). It was soon realised that both faeces output and herbage digestibility might be estimated by the use of so-called indicator (marker) techniques.

Indicators are generally substances that are completely indigestible; those used in grazing experiments fall into two categories:
(a) substances given to animals in **known quantity**, either directly (eg as a pill) or by addition to the feed,
(b) components of the feed, present in **known concentration**.

Indicators of type (a) are used to measure faecal output, an example being the inert and indigestible substance, chromium sesquioxide (Cr_2O_3; "chromic oxide"). If an animal is given a constant quantity daily (c g day^{-1}), it will on average excrete the same quantity daily. If a small sample of faeces is collected from the animal and found to contain f g Cr_2O_3 kg DM^{-1} then faecal DM output (F kg day^{-1}) can be calculated as:

$$F = c/f \tag{1.2}$$

Indicators of type (b) are used to estimate digestibility, an example being lignin. As a feed passes through an animal, its lignin concentration is progressively increased by removal of other constituents through digestion and absorption; the overall increase in concentration (ie the difference between concentrations in feed and faeces) is proportional to feed digestibility. Thus the digestibility coefficient of feed dry matter (D) may be calculated from the concentrations of lignin in feed (1_i) and faeces (1_o) by the equation:

$$D = (1_o - 1_i)/1_o \tag{1.3}$$

It should be noted that chromic oxide was originally used as a type (b) indicator with feeds into which it could be intimately mixed (Edin, 1926), but for grazing studies any type (b) indicator must be a natural constituent. Chromic oxide was first used as a type (a) indicator for grazing animals at the Ruakura Animal Research Station in 1948 (Coup, 1950). Silica had been used much earlier as a type (b) indicator to estimate the digestibility of hay (Wildt, 1874), but the first indicator of this type to be used in grazing experiments was lignin (Forbes and Garrigus, 1948). Blaxter (1948) gave the first report of type (a) and (b) indicators being used together to estimate the intake of grazing animals; the substances used were barium sulphate and lignin. The introduction and development of techniques based on other indicators is described in later chapters.

The use of chromic oxide to estimate faeces output has continued until the present day, although the technique has been recognised as not fully satisfactory and has therefore been explored and modified in a variety of ways (see Chapter 3). The basic problems in the use of chromic oxide are firstly, that the quantity administered is sometimes incompletely recovered in faeces (for reasons still unknown), and secondly, that the administration of discrete doses of the indicator (perhaps once or twice a day) leads to diurnal variations in the concentration of the indicator in faeces, and hence to difficulty in estimating the mean concentration from faeces samples taken once or twice daily.

The use of the ratio indicators to estimate digestibility in the manner described above (Equation 1.3) was discontinued when it was realised that the accuracy of this method depended on the concentration of the indicator in the herbage being the same in the feed sample collected by cutting or "plucking" the sward as in the herbage consumed by the grazing animal. As animals generally exercise some degree of selectivity, even when grazing apparently uniform swards, the method became suspect. It should be noted in passing that the method of Garrigus (1934) was open to the same criticism.

The next development in the estimation of digestibility was the faecal index method (Gallup et al, 1940; Lancaster, 1949). It was found that if a series of digestibility trials with cut herbages was carried out, a relationship could be demonstrated between the organic matter digestibility of the herbage and the concentration in faeces of nitrogen (N). Later, some of the ratio indicators, such as plant pigments or fibre, were also used as faecal index substances. Equations describing the relationships could then be used to estimate digestibility in the grazing animal solely by analysis of its faeces. The subsequent widespread use of faecal index techniques duly exposed imperfections which have led to their decline. The basic problem is that for any one indicator, such as nitrogen, there is no single equation describing the relationship of its faecal concentration to herbage digestibility which is uniformly applicable to the multifarious combinations of plant and animal species encountered in grazing experiments. Essentially, it was found necessary to recalibrate the relationship for any particular grazing situation, which meant that grazing trials had to be accompanied by indoor digestibility trials, as carried out by Garrigus (1934). Again, the problems of faecal index methods are discussed in Chapter 3.

At this point, there occurred a development which allowed a return to the simpler methods of estimating digestibility used by Garrigus (1934) and the advocates of the ratio methods. This was the use of the oesophageal fistula to permit representative sampling of herbage "as grazed". It was first used by Torell (1954) and initially the samples obtained were analysed for ratio indicators. Later, the introduction of reliable methods to estimate digestibility *in vitro* (Tilley and Terry, 1963) allowed more direct use of the samples. Despite problems in its general application (see Chapter 3 again) sampling herbage via an oesophageal fistula is now the preferred route to the estimation of the digestibility of grazed herbage.

This brief, historical review of methods used to measure intake would be incomplete without reference to some approximate methods which may be used in special circumstances. Chacon *et al* (1976) counted the number of bites taken by grazing dairy cows, and estimated bite size from material collected from an oesophageal fistula; the two measures were then combined to provide estimates of intake (see Chapter 6). Harumoto and Kato (1978) have suggested that ruminating time can be used as an index of herbage intake. Intake estimates may also be obtained from animal production data by the reverse use of feeding standards, as described in Chapter 4; although such estimates are of little value in nutritional studies they may be more useful in estimating the amount of herbage consumed under different grazing management conditions.

1.3 THE PLACE OF INTAKE MEASUREMENTS IN GRAZING EXPERIMENTS

A common feature of most methods for measuring intake is that they are laborious, and therefore expensive to use. Dosing 20 beef cattle twice daily with chromic oxide and collecting faecal samples *per rectum*, for example, can take two men 3 h per day, and the samples must subsequently be mixed and analysed. A concurrent digestibility trial with cut herbage, or alternatively, the frequent sampling from (and maintenance of) animals with oesophageal fistulae, will add considerably to this work load. Furthermore, the dependence of the methods on faecal sampling or collection makes the routine work somewhat unpleasant. There is therefore a strong temptation for the experimenter to simplify methods and routines until their precision is impaired. Too few animals may be used, sampling periods may be too short, a ready made faecal index regression may be employed instead of one derived especially for the experiment. As a result, the estimates of intake may be so biased or imprecise as to be worthless. A rule suggested for measurements of intake is that such measurements should not be made unless (a) a definite requirement for them can be established, and (b) they can be made with a degree of accuracy appropriate to the needs of the experiment.

Reference was made earlier to a hypothetical experiment in which pure stands of two herbage cultivars were grazed, and animal production was recorded. If animal production differed between the cultivars, measurements of herbage intake (and of digestibility) would subsequently be needed to explain this difference. This raises the question as to whether the experimenter should have anticipated the difference in performance, and hence the need to explain it, and should therefore have included measurement of herbage intake in his comparison right at the start. The answer may well depend on the experimenter's expectations. Many comparisons of herbage cultivars (or of management practices such as strip and continuous grazing) show no differences in animal production. One may therefore argue that intake measurements made in such cases are of little value except insofar as they may support the observations of similar production. Because of the cost and complexity of intake measurements, it is suggested that such measurements should not be made unless there are good grounds for supposing that the treatments will cause differences in other parameters, such as measures of animal performance. Thus, if the experimenter was working with new and previously untested herbage varieties he would be well advised to begin his study with a relatively simple and undemanding comparison of animal performance, and to be prepared to follow this with a more detailed study that included measurement of intake.

An important requirement of experiments involving intake measurements is that the logic of the comparisons made, and the design employed, should be faultless. In some of the earlier investigations of grazing systems, for example, different stocking rates were used for the systems being compared. This led to erroneous conclusions concerning animal production per unit area, but it is unlikely that the inclusion of intake measurements in these investigations would have led to a more accurate assessment of the various systems. Although intake measurements may add depth to an otherwise superficial experiment, they cannot make up for poor logic. When considering the experimental design the investigator should bear in mind that the major source of random error in estimates of intake is the between-animal variation in appetite, not the errors of estimate arising from the imprecision of the methods employed; this can be seen, for example, in experiments in which intake of zero-grazed herbage (measured directly) has been compared with intake of the same herbage grazed in the field and estimated by indicator methods (eg Greenhalgh & Runcie, 1962). The effects of real differences between animals in intake (and also in production) on experimental error may be minimised by employing

changeover designs or those involving periods of uniform treatment of the
animals (eg Greenhalgh *et al*, 1966). If such designs are not applicable much
greater efforts will be needed to estimate intake precisely.

While the random errors of methods for estimating intake may be
relatively unimportant, biases introduced by these methods are always a
hazard. If chromic oxide excretion is less than the intake of the indicator,
faeces output and intake will both be over-estimated. Regression equations
relating digestibility to faecal N concentration will generally have quite large
residual standard errors, but when these equations are used in experiments
to predict the former from the latter, the error terms are usually ignored.
Variation in predicted digestibility for, say, individual animals within a
treatment group, will then depend solely on variation in faecal N
concentration (which is generally small). The predictions are thus given an
air of great precision which may hide the fact that, for reasons discussed
earlier, they may all be biased. Poor precision, meaning large random errors
is self-evident, but poor accuracy, meaning bias, may go undetected unless
checking procedures are built into the experiment (for example, chromic
oxide recovery might be checked by total collection of faeces from some
animals).

It is always worth remembering that intake is more easily and accurately
measured with housed livestock than with grazing animals, and that a
"grazing" experiment carried out indoors (zero grazing) with cut herbage
(fresh, formic-acid preserved, frozen or even dried) may provide much
useful information (see Chapter 5). While some aspects of grassland
utilisation, such as the influence of management systems, or the energy cost
to the animal of grazing a particularly sparse sward, must be investigated
with animals grazing in the field, many nutritional comparisons may lose
little in verisimilitude and gain much in precision if moved indoors. There is
a tendency to assume that if contrasting pasture species, or even cultivars
within a species, are compared by zero-grazing, the differences between
them in intake, digestibility and animal production will not be the same as
those that might be recorded with field grazing, but there is a lack of
experimental evidence on this topic. Furthermore, an experiment carried
out in the field under "natural" conditions is still a compromise, because its
constant features — such as stocking rate, fertilizer use, etc — must be
chosen somewhat arbitrarily from the many permutations possible. There is
no particular merit in carrying out an experiment in the often difficult
circumstances of field grazing if more reliable and no less relevant
information can be got from an indoor feeding trial.

1.4 CONCLUSIONS

Measurements of the intake of grazed herbage should not be introduced into an experiment without giving the matter a good deal of thought. The questions to be asked are of the kind: Are there good reasons for expecting treatment differences in intake? Is the experiment sufficiently well designed and constructed to justify the use of the complex methodology required? Are there enough resources available to ensure the correct application of methods, so that biases, in particular, are not introduced? Would a zero-grazing experiment be a better alternative? And finally, if it is decided to go ahead and measure intake, are the methods available likely to be successful in the particular circumstances of the experiment?

Once a decision has been taken to attempt the measurement of intake, the methods available must be carefully considered in relation to the conditions of the experiment. For example, the techniques used to measure the intake of dairy cows grazed intensively on uniform lowland swards can be simpler than those used for sheep ranging over a large area of hill pasture. It is not enough to justify the use of inadequate methods on the grounds that they are "the best available", if only because reservations made in the planning phase of the experiment may be forgotten later if the methods do in fact, produce plausible results. Inaccurate estimates of intake will not advance the science of grassland utilisation, and may retard progress by diverting resources to their re-investigation.

The approach to intake measurements followed in this chapter — cautious, critical and even pessimistic — has been chosen deliberately to encourage the reader to take an equally critical view. The measurement of herbage intake is not easy in even the best of pastoral conditions and becomes quite impossible in difficult circumstances; if it were not so, there would be no need for this book. Nevertheless, the reader should not allow caution totally to repress enthusiasm. There is a great deal to be learned about the intake of grazing animals and there is plenty of scope for improving the methodology of intake measurement.

1.5 REFERENCES

BLAXTER, K L (1948). See WATSON, S J (1948). Animals as a means of evaluating pasture production. *Proceedings of the British Society of Animal Production*, p 38.

CHACON, E, STOBBS, T H and SANDLAND, R L (1976). Estimation of herbage consumption by grazing cattle using measurements of eating behaviour. *Journal of the British Grassland Society*, 31, 81-87.

COUP, M R (1950). The measurement of faeces output. *Proceedings of the New Zealand Society of Animal Production*, 10, 43-44.

EDIN, H (1926). Forsatta försök med indirekta p) "ledkroppsprincipen" grundader metoder för bestämning av fodrets smältbarhet. Krom oxid som "ledkropp" (kvantitativ indikator). (Preliminary experiment on the indirect method for determination of forage digestibility by the indicator principle. Chromic oxide as a quantitative indicator). *Fran Centralanstalten för Försöksväsandet på jordbruksområdet. Husdjursavdelningen* No 50, Med 309. Stockholm.

ERIZIAN, E (1932). Eine neue Methode zur Bestimmung der vom Vieh gefressenen Menge Weidefutters. (A new method for estimation of the quantity of pasture eaten by cattle). *Zeitschrift fur Zuchtungsbiologie, Reihe B25, 443-459.*

FORBES, R M and GARRIGUS, W P (1948). Application of a lignin ratio technique to the determination of the nutrient intake of grazing animals. *Journal of Animal Science,* 7, 373-382.

GALLUP, W D, HOBBS, C S and BRIGGS, H M (1945). The use of silica as a reference substance in digestion trials with ruminants. *Journal of Animal Science,* 4, 68-71.

GARRIGUS, W P (1934). The forage consumption of grazing steers. *Proceedings of the American Society of Animal Production,* p 66.

GREENHALGH, J F D (1969). Herbage quality in the field. In Grass and Forage Breeding (ed I Phillips and R Hughes). *Occasional Symposium of the British Grassland Society,* No 5.

GREENHALGH, J F D and RUNCIE, K V (1962). The herbage intake and milk production of strip- and zero-grazed dairy cows. *Journal of Agricultural Science, Cambridge,* 59, 95–103.

GREENHALGH, J F D, REID, G W, AITKEN, J N and FLORENCE, E (1966). The effects of grazing intensity on herbage consumption and animal production. I. Short-term effects in strip-grazed dairy cows. *Journal of Agricultural Science, Cambridge,* 67, 13-23.

HARUMOTO, T and KATO, M (1978). Use of ruminating time as an index of herbage intake by grazing animals. *Journal of the Japanese Society of Grassland Science,* 24, 232-238.

LANCASTER, R J (1949). Estimation of digestibility of grazed pasture from faeces nitrogen. *Nature, London,* 163, 330-331.

MacLUSKY, D S (1955). The quantities of herbage eaten by grazing dairy cows. *Proceedings of the British Society of Animal Production,* pp 45-51.

TILLEY, J M A and TERRY, R A (1963). A two-stage technique for the *in vitro* digestion of forage crops. *Journal of the British Grassland Society,* 18, 104-111.

TORELL, D T (1954). An esophageal fistula for animal nutrition studies. *Journal of Animal Science,* 13, 878-884.

WATSON, S J (1948). Animals as means of evaluating pasture production. *Proceedings of the British Society of Animal Production,* pp 7-43

WILDT, H (1874). *Journal für Landwirtschaft,* 22, 1.

WOODMAN, H E, EVANS, R E and EDEN, A (1937). Sheep nutrition. II. Determination of the amounts of grass consumed by sheep on pasturage of varying quality. *Journal of Agricultural Science, Cambridge,* 27, 212-223.

CHAPTER 2

SWARD METHODS

J.A.C. Meijs, R.J.K. Walters and A. Keen

2.1 INTRODUCTION

Sward methods for measuring herbage intake are based on the same principle as for indoor experiments where intake is measured by difference:

herbage intake = herbage offered — herbage refused

The herbage mass (total mass of herbage per unit area of ground) is estimated at the beginning and at the end of the grazing period. The difference between the two gives an estimate of the apparent quantity of herbage consumed per unit area, but since the herbage may also grow during the grazing period a correction has to be applied to allow for this. The calculated consumption per unit area is then converted to intake per animal per day by dividing by the number of animal-days per unit area.

The measurement of herbage mass at the beginning and end of the grazing period can be achieved with reasonable accuracy, but the accurate measurement of herbage that may accumulate during grazing presents greater problems. Consequently, sward sampling methods are mainly applicable in systems where the grazing periods are relatively short, and where grazing pressures are high (ie paddock, or strip grazing systems). Under these circumstances the amount of herbage that may accumulate during grazing will form only a relatively small proportion of the total herbage consumption, thus minimising the possibility of bias in estimating intake.

Sward methods can only provide intake data on an individual-animal basis where animals are kept in individual plots. However, to obtain a normal grazing behaviour pattern and to reduce the labour requirement, intake studies are usually carried out with groups of animals. An advantage of the sward method is that the measurements also provide information on the herbage allowance (the weight of herbage per unit of animal live weight) and the efficiency of grazing (herbage consumed expressed as a proportion of the herbage accumulated). In addition, chemical analysis of the samples taken allows pasture quality to be measured.

Methods of estimating herbage mass can be classified as destructive (cutting) or non-destructive. Cutting techniques usually involve the harvesting of a measured proportion of the area of pasture allotted to the animals and weighing and sampling the cut herbage. The amount of residual herbage (that remaining after grazing) is similarly determined. Non-destructive techniques usually involve the measurement of one or more sward characteristics in the grazing area before and after grazing, combined with a prediction of the herbage mass using an appropriate regression equation. This involves taking a limited number of cut samples to correlate with the sward characteristic.

The potential for sward cutting techniques to provide reliable intake estimates depends on eliminating or minimising:
— possible systematic errors in estimating the difference between herbage mass at the start of grazing and at the end of grazing arising from the measurement technique.
— possible systematic errors in estimating the herbage accumulation during the grazing period.
— the random variation of the intake estimate, the precision of estimates depending on the variation in herbage mass within the pasture, on the method of sampling, and on the number, size and shape of the sample units.

The potential for non-destructive techniques to provide reliable intake estimates depends in addition on the possible systematic or random errors which may arise when applying the regression equation obtained between a variable (eg sward height) and the herbage mass, to estimate the mass of the pasture as a whole.

Reviews of literature on the subject of sward-methods have been made by Brown (1954), C.A.B. (1961), Carter (1962), 't Mannetje (1978), Frame (1981) and Meijs (1981). Frame (1981) gives information on sources of equipment for a range of sward sampling procedures. The intention in this chapter is; a) to give detailed descriptions of sward methods (including requirement for equipment and labour), b) to make a critical evaluation of the possible systematic and random errors, and c) to make an assessment of the relevance of the various methods available for particular experimental objectives.

2.2 METHODS OF ESTIMATING HERBAGE MASS

2.2.1 Sward-cutting techniques

The suitability of machinery for herbage sampling depends on the intended height of cutting, which in turn depends on the expected height of grazing. Therefore a division will be made into three categories of cutting techniques based on their suitability for estimating intake in different situations (Table 2.1).

Table 2.1   Classification of three cutting techniques

	Approximate cutting height	Type	Grazing pressure
Cutting at field-scale mowing level	5 cm	Cattle grazing	Low/moderate
Cutting at lawnmower level	3 cm	Cattle grazing	Moderate/high
		Sheep grazing	Low
Cutting close to ground level	0 cm	Cattle grazing	High
		Sheep grazing	High

2.2.1.1 *Cutting at field-scale mowing level.* Motorscythes are often used for sampling crops intended for conservation at those stubble heights obtained in farm practice. Such machines usually cut at a height of 4.5–5 cm and can vary in fingerbar width from 60 to 120 cm. They have a reciprocating knife which is actuated by a central rocker arm and can cut a swath with clearly defined edges without damaging the crop. Allen autoscythes and Agria motorscythes are often used for estimating intake in grazing experiments. Their value is largely limited to situations where herbage growth is erect and grazing intensity is relatively low.

After cutting, the material has to be raked and put into containers, eg plastic bags. The length of the strips can be measured with a tape. The labour requirement per paddock, plot or field depends on the size, number and distribution of the sample units used. In experiments of Meijs (1981), 10 strips, 60 cm wide and 12 m long were cut per paddock (0.3 ha) with an Agria motorscythe at the start of each grazing period. The total field labour requirement when 10 strips were cut was approximately 1.5 man-hours (cutting 0.5, raking + collecting 0.75, measuring cut area 0.25 man-hours). Less time is needed to collect the smaller residues of post-grazing strips, but this is counter-balanced by the time required for removing faeces from the sampling area to be cut.

Advantages of this cutting height are:

a) comparability of herbage mass with that of herbage cut for conservation

b) minimal soil contamination

c) minimal damage to the sward.

Disadvantages include the possibility of introducing bias due to:

a) failure to sample below grazing height (especially at high levels of grazing intensity)

b) flattening of herbage to below cutting height due to trampling, lying down of animals, faeces contamination and cutting or raking action

c) difference in cutting height between start and finish of grazing.

Several experiments have been reported indicating bias due to a), and some information concerning b) and c) was reported by Meijs (1981). In his studies the height of the stubble of the post-grazing strips was 0.43 cm longer than that of the pre-grazing strips, thus indicating the occurrence of bias b) and/or c). The stubble mass after cutting pre- and post-grazing strips with a motorscythe was compared by cutting the same strips again with a lawnmower (cutting width 50 cm, cutting height 3.1 or 3.5 cm, depending on type of machine). The stubble mass of the post-grazing strips cut by the lawnmower was on average 155 kg ha^{-1} of organic matter higher than that of the pre-grazing strips (Table 2.2). Without correction the herbage intake would thus have been overestimated by 10%.

It is not advisable to use a motorscythe when absolute levels of intake have to be estimated due to such possible systematic errors. However, if these errors are likely to be similar for different treatments, it is possible to satisfactorily estimate relative differences in intake between treatments.

2.2.1.2 *Cutting at lawnmower level.* Lawnmowers are not suitable for cutting tall vegetation and they can result in considerable losses of herbage due to difficulties in collecting the cut material (Hardy *et al*, 1978). To overcome these problems a two-step cutting system has been developed by Meijs

(1981) and Schlepers (personal communication 1978). Strips of herbage are first cut with a reciprocating motormower as described (2.2.1.1), and after removing the cut herbage a lawnmower with a narrower mowing width is used to cut the same strips (Table 2.2).

Table 2.2   Estimation of herbage mass (organic matter) with motorscythe and lawnmower (Meijs, 1981).

Cutting equipment	Motorscythe	Lawnmower	Motorscythe and lawnmower
Cutting height (cm), start of grazing	4.51	3.33	3.33
Herbage mass, start of grazing (kg ha^{-1})	2140	457	2597
Residual herbage, end of grazing (kg ha^{-1})	754	612	1366
Difference (kg ha^{-1})	1386	−155	1231

Two types of lawnmowers have been used; Husqvarna (cutting width 48 cm, cutting height 3.5 cm) and Honda (cutting width 51 cm, cutting height 3.1 cm). They have a rotary action and collect the cut material by suction into a box behind the machine. To correct for soil contamination all data must be expressed on an organic matter basis. The collecting box of the Honda lawnmower contains a plastic liner bag which can be changed quickly after cutting each strip. The total field labour requirement per paddock (10 strips) for the cutting and collecting work with the motorscythe and lawnmower is approximately 2 man-hours. Cutting with both machines ensures a constant cutting height and stubble mass for pre- and postgrazing sample strips, if weather conditions during pre- and postgrazing are comparable. Further studies indicated that under very wet conditions the cutting efficiency of both machines was reduced and the stubble mass increased. Thus systematic errors in estimating intake may be introduced by a difference in weather conditions during pre- and postgrazing sampling.

The additional advantages of the two-step cutting system are:

a)   reproducible cutting height and stubble mass for pre- and postgrazing strips

b)   little chance of root material contaminating the sample.

Disadvantages of the two-step cutting system include:

a)   a relative high labour requirement both in the field and in the laboratory (2 herbage samples per strip)

b)   animals (particularly sheep) may graze below sampling height.

2.2.1.3 *Cutting close to ground level.* Total herbage mass can be estimated with hand-held equipment. The simplest cutting devices are hand-operated tools such as shears, scissors and knives. These require a high labour input but have the advantage that height of cutting can be accurately controlled especially when rough or trampled areas are to be harvested. However, individuals can vary in the height they consider representative of ground level. Therefore it is advisable that pre- and postgrazing strips are sampled by the same operator.

To reduce labour requirements, hand-held power-driven tools such as hedge trimmers and sheep-shearing hand pieces are commonly used. Hedge-trimmers have the following disadvantages:

a) they do not cut at ground level and are not generally equipped with collecting trays

b) postgrazing samples may be cut to a lower level than pre-grazing samples (Alder and Minson, 1963)

c) they require frequent overhaul and replacement of cutter-bar assemblies.

The sheep-shearing head is less difficult to maintain in good cutting order and is capable of cutting closer to ground level than the hedge trimmer. Reliable results can be obtained with an electrically operated sheep-shearing head (eg Sunbeam Stewart shearmaster) fitted with a standard 7.62 cm comb and cutter, and powered by a mobile generator (110 V) fitted with a 20 m extension lead (Walters and Evans, 1979). Within each paddock six pre- and six postgrazing strips, each measuring approximately 7.6 cm wide and 25 m long, are cut as close to ground level as possible taking care to avoid undue soil contamination.

Taking 6 sample strips per paddock (0.05 ha) requires approximately 1 man-hour. For ten strips (eg on an area of 0.3 ha comparable with the paddocks used with the cutting machinery as described in 2.2.1.1 and 2.2.1.2) the labour requirement is about 1.7 man-hours.

Advantages of the sheep-shearing head are:

a) no herbage can be grazed below the cutting level

b) a reproducible cutting height before and after grazing can be achieved.

General disadvantages are:

a) comparison with estimates of herbage mass harvested at different times during the season by a machine cutting for conservation is difficult, and may preclude the possibility of calculating whole season yields

b) high level of soil contamination

c)   damage to the sward.

Under certain conditions the following difficulties have been encountered when using the sheep-shearing head:

a)   on uneven ground some root growth may be cut and included in the sample, and under these conditions samples cut with cordless grass shears may be preferable to the shearing head (Matches, 1963)

b)   the amount of dead organic material included in the sample may vary depending on weather conditions

c)   losses can occur in recovering post-grazed samples from swards showing a prostrate habit of growth

d)   overestimation of the factor for calculating herbage accumulation during grazing.

To avoid problems due to differential soil contamination all herbage mass data should be expressed on an organic matter basis.

2.2.1.4   *Comparison between cutting methods.* A comparison and summary of the important aspects of the three cutting equipment categories is shown in Table 2.3. Due to the high risk of bias, it is not advisable to use the motorscythe as the sole machine when estimating absolute levels of intake. By comparison the risk of bias using the other cutting equipment is likely to be low.

Table 2.3   Comparison of cutting machinery

References	Meijs (1981)		Walters and Evans (1979)
Cutting equipment	Motorscythe	Motorscythe + Lawnmower	Sheep-shearing head
Cutting height (cm)	4.51	3.33	±0
Cutting width (m)	0.60	0.50	0.08
Cutting length (m)	12	12	25
Cutting area per strip (m^2)	7.2	6.0	2.0
Labour requirement in the field per paddock (10 samples in man hours)	1.5	2.0	1.7
Avoiding grazing below cutting height	−	+	+
Achieving comparable stubble pre/post	−	+	+
Comparability with field-scale mowing	+	+	−
Low soil contamination	+	±	−
Little damage to the sward	+	+	−
Calculating accumulation factor (2.3)	+	+	−

− = negative aspect
+ = positive aspect

The two-step cutting system allows a large area to be sampled in a relatively short period of time (see Table 2.3). Field labour is only a part of the total labour requirement which also includes transporting, weighing, sub-sampling and analysing the samples. With the two-step system, two samples per sample unit have to be weighed and ashed whereas with the sheep-shearing head only one sample per unit is generated. Both methods are suitable for intensively managed swards, the choice depends on the experimental circumstances:– ie the available labour supply, the type of grazing animal, the intensity of grazing, the likelihood of damaging the pasture, the need to calculate seasonal yields in alternating cutting/grazing trials, and the level of precision required.

2.2.2 Non-destructive techniques

The various non-destructive techniques have been reviewed by Brown (1954), Frame (1981) and 't Mannetje (1978) and may be classified as follows:

a)   eye estimations

b)   height and density measurements

c)   non-vegetative attributes.

2.2.2.1 *Eye estimations.* Two methods of estimating herbage mass by visual appraisal can be identified. In the first the observer makes a large number of observations throughout the pasture following a period of intensive training based on repeated checks by cutting and weighing (Pechanec & Pickford, 1937). Alternatively one of the sampling systems using concomitant variables can be adopted (see 2.4.1.3). With double sampling it is recommended that two observers are used per pasture and that each observer develops his own calibration curve to minimise the possibility of observer bias (Haydock & Shaw, 1975). A refinement of this method for use in short intensively grazed pastures has been developed by Hutchinson *et al* (1972) which involves taking a limited number (eg 8) of cores (10 cm diameter) from the pasture to represent the full range of levels of herbage mass present. The herbage on the cores is then scored for mass and the cores are arranged on a circular tray in an ordered sequence. The tray is then carried by the observer when scoring the pasture, and the cores are used as a visual aid. When pasture scoring has been completed the herbage on each reference core is cut and weighed, and a regression equation is calculated to convert scores to yield.

The sources of bias (exclusive of bias in cutting the reference areas which has already been dealt with in section 2.2.1) include a) insufficient training — untrained observers tend to overestimate tall growing swards and underestimate dense swards. b) idiosynchrosy of observers — some observers, although trained, tend to persistently over- or underestimate herbage mass, c) fatigue — after prolonged periods eg over 3 hours of intensive pasture examination, observers tend to over- or underestimate mass.

Depending on the size and heterogeneity of pastures, training and calibration can take up to 2 man-hours per pasture. Pasture scores following training can be made at the rate of 1 every 30 seconds.

2.2.2.2 *Height and/or density measurements.* Herbage mass is estimated from the separate measurements of height and/or density after having first calibrated these parameters against actual herbage mass by cutting and weighing, using a system of double sampling. Height is normally defined as maximum or mean and is measured by a ruler. Density is defined as percentage ground cover and is estimated by point quadrat or visual appraisal (Bakhuis, 1960). Alternatively, the weighted disc grassmeter (eg Earle and McGowan, 1979) is used which provides an integrated measurement of height and density. This technique represents a considerable advance in precision, accuracy, speed of operation and convenience over the separate measurements of height and density.

The main sources of bias additional to those concerned with cutting reference areas include, a) sward structure, b) lodged or trampled herbage, c) botanical composition, d) season, e) grazing management.

Depending on the size and heterogeneity of pastures, calibration can take from 30 minutes to 4 hours. The shorter time applies when the weighted disc meter is used whilst the longer time applies when both height and density are measured as separate parameters. The random pasture measurements made with the ruler, point quadrat or grassmeter are rapid, eg a measurement every 10-20 seconds.

2.2.2.3 *Measurement of non-vegetative attributes.* Herbage mass can be estimated from one of a number of non-vegetative plant attributes (eg capacitance, radioisotope attenuation, spectral analysis) after having first calibrated the respective parameter with actual herbage mass by cutting and weighing. Of these methods, capacitance has been most intensively studied and forms the subject of this section.

The principle and range of meters developed for measuring capacitance have been reviewed by Neal and Neal (1973). The meter measures the change in capacitance caused by introducing vegetation into a capacitance system. Ideally the change in capacitance is directly proportional to herbage mass and is registered on a dial fitted to the measuring head of the meter.

This type of meter is of a "multiple probe" design, and research experience has generally shown that this design has severe limitations in providing reliable herbage mass data due to the many extraneous factors that can influence meter readings (Angelone *et al*, 1980a). An alternative meter design has been proposed by Nomoto (1975), and more recently by Angelone *et al* 1980b), in an attempt to overcome these problems.

In the double sampling method described by Jones & Haydock (1970) (see 2.4.1.3) the sources of bias include a) moisture content, b) conductance, c) botanical composition, d) sward structure, e) sward density, f) season, g) evenness of soil surface, h) ratio of green: dead material etc. The calibration of the meter can take up to 2-3 hours per pasture, followed by subsequent random readings which can be taken about every 2 minutes.

2.2.2.4 *Comparison between non-destructive and cutting methods.* Potential advantages of non-destructive methods over cutting methods for estimating herbage mass include:

a)   greater speed of operation

b)   lower labour requirements

c)   no residual pasture damage

d)   greater ease of operation far from base or in difficult terrain.

The non-destructive techniques described, however, are subject to greater error (see 2.4.3.2) and are more liable to bias than cutting methods. Higher error can be mitigated to some extent by increasing the number of observations per unit area made possible by the greater speed of operation of these techniques, but their liability to bias is more difficult to resolve. Consequently, it is recommended when using these techniques that regular and frequent calibrations are made to minimise this possibility. Unbiased non-destructive methods (see 2.4.1.3) are also possible, but these do not have the same advantages in ease of operation as the systematic non-destructive methods described here. An assessment of the relative advantages and disadvantages of methods, based on experience at the Welsh Plant Breeding Station is given in Table 2.4.

At their present stage of development none of the non-destructive techniques can be regarded as critical research methods for estimating intake, due mainly to their liability to bias. At best they can provide a rough guide to grazing intake where pastures are relatively homogeneous and conditions are uniform, and where large differences are expected in herbage mass between the start and end of grazing. However, in all cases results should be treated with caution.

Table 2.4   Relative advantages (v) and disadvantages (x) of non-destructive and cutting methods for estimating herbage mass.

	Cutting methods	Non-destructive methods		
		Height/ density (disc meter)	Visual	Non-vegetative attributes (capacitance)
Speed of operation	xx	vvv	vvv	v
Labour requirements	x	vv	vvv	vv
Equipment requirements (cost)	x	vvv	vv	v
Convenience	xx	vvv	vvv	vv
Pasture damage	xxx	vvv	vvv	vvv
Precision	vvv	x	x	xx
Liable to bias	vvv	xx	xx	xxx

2.3 ACCUMULATION OF HERBAGE DURING THE GRAZING PERIOD

The sward cutting technique is mainly applicable when the grazing period is short and relatively large amounts of material are eaten per unit area during the period. In this situation herbage accumulation during the period of grazing (disturbed accumulation) is negligible in relation to the total amount of herbage consumed and can thus be reasonably ignored when calculating intake. However, when grazing takes place over an extended period (more than one day), herbage accumulation during grazing cannot be ignored. The disturbed accumulation is difficult to measure since it is constantly being influenced by the grazing animal. It is therefore normally measured indirectly from an estimate of the rate of undisturbed herbage accumulation (in exclosures) during grazing. This estimate is then used to calculate disturbed accumulation using a model relating disturbed and undisturbed accumulation.

An estimate of the rate of undisturbed accumulation during grazing can be calculated from estimates of the herbage mass at the beginning and at the end of the grazing period as follows:

a) Under cages (one sample in each cage).
Cages are commonly 4.20 m long and 1.2 m wide; more details about design and materials used are given by Brown (1954). Bias may arise if herbage is protected by a cage for any length of time due to the protection from grazing and the abnormal microclimate within the cage resulting in a herbage accumulation not typical for the rest of the sward. The magnitude of this effect is directly related to the length of time the cages are in a given position ('t Mannetje, 1978). If the grazing period is shorter than one week this effect is insignificant. A disadvantage of

cages is their fixed size, especially if it is intended that sample unit should take the form of long strips. Another possible disadvantage is their influence on the behaviour of the animals possibly leading to sward damage in the vicinity of the cages.

b) In fenced areas (allowing several samples from each fenced area).
    Often one or two areas are fenced off within the pasture and in each exclosure a number of samples are cut. Advantages of using large fenced-off areas include a wider choice of the area to cut at each sample site (this is especially important when cutting is mechanized) and minimal bias since the effect of fencing on microclimate of the sward exclosures is negligible. As a result of fencing-off only one or a few relatively large parts of the grazed area there is a possibility of siting the exclosures in non-representative areas of the pasture. However, since absolute measurements of herbage mass are not required this should not create a serious problem. When the sward in the exclosures has reached a certain leaf area index (about 5.7) herbage accumulation (undisturbed) is almost independent of level of herbage mass, thus reducing the possibility of bias due to non-representative siting of exclosures.

The disturbed herbage accumulation in the grazed area will be lower than the undisturbed accumulation in the exclosure due to defoliation (reduction of leaf area per unit area), treading, and faeces contamination. Thus, disturbed accumulation = g x undisturbed accumulation. The herbage consumed when a correction is applied for the disturbed herbage accumulation can then be calculated:

$$C = M\text{-}M^f + g.\triangle M^e \qquad (2.1)$$

C = herbage consumed (kg ha^{-1})
M = herbage mass at the start of a grazing period (kg ha^{-1})
M^f = residual herbage at the end of a grazing period (kg ha^{-1})
$\triangle M^e$ = undisturbed herbage accumulation in exclosure during a grazing period (kg ha^{-1}).

Linehan *et al* (1947) assumed that the rate of herbage accumulation and the rate of consumption of herbage were each proportional to the quantity of herbage present at a given time during the grazing period and derived the following equation:

$$C = (M\text{-}M^f) \ \frac{\log (M + \triangle M^e) - \log M^f}{\log M - \log M^f} \qquad (2.2)$$

When the formulae (2.1) and (2.2) are combined the accumulation factor g can be calculated:

$$g = \frac{(M - M^f) \log \left(\dfrac{M + \triangle M^e}{M}\right)}{(\triangle M^e) \log \dfrac{M}{M^f}} \qquad (2.3)$$

Linehan *et al* (1947) compared their sward-based estimate of intake with that calculated from liveweight gains of growing bullocks, using feeding standards in reverse. The average results showed reasonable agreement between the two methods if results were taken over a two-year period, but the difference between years varied from –27% (first year) to +18% (second year) with even greater discrepancies between individual grazing periods within years.

Bosch (1956) simplified the formula of Linehan to $g = 0.5$. He compared this with Linehan's formula and found that both equations gave similar results when the residual herbage mass was 20-30% of the herbage mass at the start of the grazing period (at a cutting level of 4 cm).

In experiments of Meijs (1981) the accumulation factor g calculated with the equation of Linehan *et al*, (1947) was on average 0.68. The reasons for this high figure were the high levels of residual herbage and the use of the two-step cutting system (in the equation of Linehan *et al*, 1947 all material above 3 cm was assumed to be photosynthetically active). If the cutting height of the motorscythe was chosen as the reference level, g was on average 0.62. However, the difference between estimates corresponds with a maximal difference of only 1.7% in herbage consumption due to the small proportion of herbage accumulation in the total herbage consumed. If herbage samples are cut at ground level the equation of Linehan *et al*, (1947) should therefore not be used.

The equation is based on the assumptions that the rate of herbage accumulation and the rate of consumption of herbage at any time during the grazing period are each proportional to the quantity of herbage remaining uneaten at that time. The first assumption has been tested (Deinum & Lantinga, personal communication 1980) and confirmed that the relationship between herbage mass and the rate of net photosynthesis was linear during the grazing period. More research is needed on the second assumption.

The relative importance of including an estimate of herbage accumulation during grazing as a component of total herbage available when measuring intake depends on:
— The length of the grazing period. At a given difference of herbage mass between beginning and end of grazing, a longer grazing period will increase the proportion of disturbed accumulation as a fraction of intake.

— The rate of herbage accumulation in the ungrazed areas. Walters and Evans (1979) calculated low organic matter accumulation rates for ungrazed swards (20 kg ha^{-1} day^{-1}) in dry periods and found adjusted values for intake (3 day grazing period, corrected with the formula of Linehan) only 3% higher than unadjusted values. In experiments of Meijs (1981) however, the average organic matter accumulation rates were high (110 kg ha^{-1} day^{-1}). On average 17% of the calculated intake using Linehan's formula consisted of disturbed herbage accumulation when grazing periods of 3-4 days were used. In spring higher accumulation rates may occur and the accumulation mass will be an even greater fraction of total intake.
— The level of herbage mass at the start and ar the finish of the grazing period. For a given grazing period the lower the level of intake, the greater will be the disturbed accumulation as a fraction of intake. At a given level of herbage mass at the start of the grazing period a higher level of herbage mass at the end of grazing will increase the factor g of Linehan.

If accurate, absolute levels of intake are required it is therefore advisable to include an estimate of herbage accumulation during grazing when grazing periods are longer than one day and when the herbage accumulation in exclosures is high, relative to the difference in herbage mass before and after grazing. If sward methods are used to estimate herbage intake, strip-grazing, or rotational grazing involving one-day paddocks are the most appropriate grazing systems to apply. However, reliable intake figures may be obtained with grazing periods of 2-4 days, provided that a correction is made relating disturbed and undisturbed accumulation. If short grazing periods are applied the proportion of disturbed accumulation as a fraction of herbage consumed is low, eg in trials of Meijs (1981) with grazing periods of 3-4 days this fraction was 17%, so a bias of 10% in the estimate of g corresponds with a bias of only 1.7% in herbage consumption. Until the equation of Linehan *et al*, (1947) has been tested over a wider range of conditions its application cannot be recommended when grazing periods exceed 5 days if absolute measurements of intake are required with a bias of less than 4% (assumed maximal bias in estimation of g is 20%).

2.4 PRECISION OF ESTIMATION OF HERBAGE MASS AND CONSUMPTION

The precision of the estimate describes how close on average the estimate is to the mean value. A measure for the precision is the standard error. The difference between the mean value of the possible estimates and the true value of the quantity to be estimated is the bias (the systematic error). Some causes of bias have been discussed in sections 2.2 and 2.3.

In many cases the 'best' estimating procedure is the one that produces a sufficiently precise estimate in the cheapest way (minimising cost of labour, machinery, laboratory), but it is important to understand the causes of variability so that the estimating procedure can be improved.

An estimate of intake derived by a sward method, is a function of estimates of the herbage mass of the pasture obtained by cutting parts of the pasture (the sampling units). The sampling procedure is the way the sampling units are selected, and the choice of the number, size and shape of these units. The precision of the estimate of the herbage mass apart from measurement error is determined by the spatial distribution of the herbage mass of the pasture (the heterogeneity of the sward) and the estimating procedure. The choice of sampling procedure has to be such that the best estimate of the herbage mass of the pasture is achieved. In estimating intake, the herbage mass of the same pasture is measured at different times and under different conditions. Therefore it is often advantageous to select the sampling units close together.

When comparing the intake for different treatments, estimates from different pastures, possibly from different groups of animals in different periods have to be used. Possible variations then also include those concerned with the intake of an animal on different pastures (with the same treatment), and in the mean intake of different groups of animals. The standard error of the estimate therefore should not be used uncritically for the comparison of treatments. From indoor experiments where the intake for separate animals can be estimated accurately, some information can be obtained about the variation in intake between animals. Also, from repetitions of intake measurements, the standard error of the estimate (including variation in intake for different pastures) can be estimated.

2.4.1 Estimation of herbage mass

2.4.1.1 *Some factors affecting variation in herbage mass and herbage intake.* The precision of the estimate of herbage mass will be adversely affected by heterogeneity of the sward. This heterogeneity is caused by variation within the pasture of factors which influence herbage accumulation, such as:

— botanical composition: large differences can exist in the accumulation of herbage between species and varieties under the same growing conditions

— soil structure and composition: the borders of a pasture may produce less herbage due to intensive treading and overriding

— supply of fertilizers and water: if the distribution of water and fertilizers is not uniform over the total grazed area, the variation in herbage mass will increase.

Towards the end of a grazing period increased heterogeneity of the sward can be caused by factors which influence herbage intake or accumulation such as:

— selection by animals between herbage species or plant parts
— selection by animals between clean and faeces contaminated herbage
— treading of herbage by the grazing animals.

The degree of selection can be decreased when lower levels of herbage allowance are applied by forcing the animals to consume less palatable herbage. The intensity of grazing thus has an influence on the variation of residual herbage. At the end of a grazing period the variation in herbage mass is higher than when the area has been cut. This variation in residual herbage and the variation in the return of nutrients by local urine and faeces excretion will increase variation in herbage mass of the re-growth. This effect can be reduced if the residual herbage is topped.

The precision of the herbage intake estimated by the sward cutting technique can be improved when using aftermath or topped pre-grazed pastures. On homogeneous swards the precision of the estimation of herbage intake can be improved with a high level of herbage mass at the beginning of grazing and a low level of residual herbage at the end of grazing.

2.4.1.2 *The spatial distribution of herbage mass.* The herbage mass at a point in the pasture can be visualised as the herbage mass per unit area in a (small) square with this point as the centre. The spatial distribution can be visualised as a contourmap, the contourlines connecting neighbouring points with the same herbage mass (Fig 2.1.).

 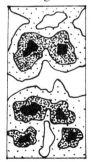 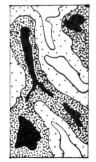 

Fig. 2.1   *Four examples of spatial distributions. The lines connect points with the same herbage mass. The darker the area the more herbage mass available.*

In practice, the spatial distribution of the herbage mass in the pasture is not known otherwise there would be no sampling problem, but some general features may be known eg whether there are trends in one or two directions (fertility, drainage pipes etc) and how rapidly the herbage mass changes between points.

2.4.1.3. *Useful types of sampling.* The type of sampling is the way the sample (ie the n units for which the measurements are to be obtained) is selected out of the total population of sampling units. Useful types are simple random sampling, stratified random sampling and systematic sampling. In these types of sampling, concomitant measures may be used to improve the estimate (these are non-destructive techniques as described in 2.2.2). Double sampling, ranked set sampling and sampling by the method of Jones and Haydock (1970) are potentially unbiased sampling techniques using concomitant measures.

Simple random sampling means selecting the n sampling units at random out of the population of possible sampling units. The estimate of the herbage mass of the pasture is the sample mean and the estimate of the population standard deviation is the sample standard deviation.

In stratified random sampling, groups of possible sampling units (the strata) in the population are formed first, followed by simple random sampling for each of the strata. The estimate of the herbage mass of the pasture is the weighted sample mean from the different strata (weighted according to the size of the strata), and the estimate of the standard deviation is the square root of the weighted mean of sample standard deviations in the different strata (weighted according to the number of samples in the strata). The best choice of stratification is where differences between strata are large and the variation between the possible units in the strata are small.

In systematic sampling the n sampling units are not selected with a random procedure, but are units at regular positions in the pasture, possibly with a random starting position. The estimate of the herbage mass is the same as with simple random sampling. There is in general no unbiased estimate of the precision. However a common estimate of the precision is the sample standard deviation, as in simple random sampling.

In double sampling a quantitative concomitant variable is measured on many randomly selected sampling units while on a few of these (the reference samples) the herbage mass is also measured. By regression the relation between the herbage mass and the concomitant variable is estimated and the regression equation is used to estimate the herbage mass on all units where the concomitant variable has been measured. Although unbiasedness of the procedure is only guaranteed if the reference samples are selected randomly, it is still advisable to select the reference samples to represent the range of levels of herbage mass present. For the estimation of herbage mass and the precision see for example MacIntyre (1978).

In ranked set sampling, k sets of k units are selected by simple random sampling (possibly within strata). The concomitant measures for these units are used to rank the units within the sets. The sampling units for which the herbage mass will be measured are the unit with rank 1 in set 1, the unit with rank 2 in set 2, etc. The whole procedure may then be repeated, say m times, so that the sample then consists of mk units. The estimate of the herbage mass is the same as with simple random sampling. The standard error of this estimate is:

$$\sqrt{\left(\frac{1}{k} \sum_{i=1}^{k} s^2_{(i)}\right)} \qquad (2.4)$$

where $s_{(i)}$ is the standard deviation of the m observations with rank i.

Jones and Haydock (1970) described a sampling method in which after first measuring a concomitant variable on a large number of randomly chosen units, the herbage mass is measured by cutting 3 units with the mean (or nearest to the mean) value for the concomitant variable. The mean of these three observations is an estimate of the mean herbage mass of the pasture. With this procedure the precision cannot be estimated.

Simple and stratified random sampling produce unbiased estimates of the herbage mass of the pasture. Systematic sampling may produce a biased estimate of the herbage mass when the regularity in the sampling scheme and the regularity in the spatial distribution coincide. If the standard deviation from a systematic sample is estimated as if it were a simple random sample, it is usually overestimated (Cochran, 1969). Nevertheless, systematic sampling is often used in practice when no estimate of the precision is needed. Selecting the sample is easily organised and in many situations it produces a precise estimate of the herbage mass.

The use of concomitant information in double sampling is advantageous when the concomitant variable is highly correlated with the herbage mass. Ranked set sampling compared with simple random sampling reduces the required sample size by a factor slightly less than ½ (k + 1), when the ranking within sets is perfect. This procedure is particularly useful if the ranking can be achieved in a simple way eg by visual inspection of the sampling units in each set.

For a reasonable choice of sampling procedure, only a global knowledge about the spatial distribution of herbage mass in the pasture is needed. Usually information on the use of the pasture in the past and of some soil characteristics is sufficient. From each experiment new information on the spatial distribution may become available, enabling (if necessary) improvements to be made in the sampling procedure.

2.4.1.4 *The size and shape of sampling units.* In general the shape of the sampling units of a given size has to be chosen in such a way that the variation in the population of sampling units is small. Practical limitations usually restrict the shape to a rectangle, ranging from a square to a very long and narrow strip. For many spatial distributions of the herbage mass, the best choice will be a long and narrow strip, placed at right angles to any trend in herbage mass.

Increasing the size of the sampling units, and choosing the shape to reduce edge effects within the practical limitations, will usually reduce the variability in the population of sampling units. When the total area sampled is constant, many small units will yield a more precise estimate of the herbage mass than a few larger ones, because the herbage mass at adjacent positions will be more alike than at distant positions. However small units require more organization and labour, with a higher cost, although laboratory costs can be reduced by combining the herbage for analysis from different small units. The best choice of shape and size therefore mainly depends on the particular local circumstances and possibilities.

The effect of the number of samples on the precision of the herbage mass estimates can be derived from the information in Section 2.4.1.3. The precision of the intake estimate is calculated as outlined in 2.4.2. If the sward method is to be applied for more years under the same circumstances it is advisable to carry out experiments so that information about the effect of the size of the sampling units on precision becomes available.

One method is to start with randomly chosen large pairs of units, subdivided into sections, in each of which the herbage mass is measured. On one unit of each pair, observations are obtained at the start, and on the other unit at the end of the grazing period. From these observations it is possible to estimate the standard errors of the estimates of herbage mass (at the beginning and end of the grazing period) and to estimate some spatial correlations. These observations also provide a better basis for choosing the sampling procedure. However, due to the variety of possible experimental designs and the complex statistical material produced it is advisable to consult a statistician during planning.

2.4.2 Estimation of intake

Two different ways of obtaining estimates of intake based on herbage mass are considered below, the procedures differing in the way the undisturbed accumulation is estimated:

system 1) cages are situated in the pasture in which the herbage mass is estimated, and measurement of the herbage mass in the cages is made at the end of the grazing period.

system 2) in a separate pasture the herbage mass is estimated at the start as
well as at the end of the grazing period.

The intake estimates are:

1) $\hat{C}_1 = \hat{M} - \hat{M}^f + g(\hat{M}^{f,e} - \hat{M}) = \hat{M}(1\text{-}g) - \hat{M}^f + g\hat{M}^{f,e}$ (2.5)

2) $\hat{C}_2 = \hat{M} - \hat{M}^f + g(\hat{M}^{f,e} - \hat{M}^e)$ (2.6)

where M is the estimate for the herbage mass (index f for finish, e for
exclosure) and g is the factor that describes the relation between disturbed
and undisturbed accumulation (see Section 2.3). The standard error of the
estimate of the intake ($\sigma_\wedge$) for a given value of g is a function of the plot
variances and correlations that can be derived by straightforward
calculations.

If the units for the estimation of the differences in herbage mass ($\triangle M$
and $\triangle M^e$) are paired the standard error of C_2 for a given value of g is:

$$\sigma_\wedge = \sqrt{[\sigma^2 \triangle M + g^2 \sigma^2 \triangle M^e]}$$ (2.7)

When applying Linehan's estimate, g is not a constant (Meijs, 1981).
Because in system 2 the exclosure is another pasture, the correlations
between $\hat{M}^{f,e}$ or $\hat{M}^e$, and $\hat{M}$ or $\hat{M}^f$ are zero. The other correlations affect the
variance of the intake estimate and therefore it is worthwhile to choose the
sampling units in such a way that the correlation between the estimates of
the herbage masses are "optimal". Two such procedures are:

a) all sampling units are randomly selected, so all correlations are zero

b) sampling units for estimating the herbage mass of the same pasture
under different conditions are situated in pairs or triples.

The variance in the population of sampling units after grazing may be
different from that in the population of sampling units before grazing.
However, the advantage of adopting different numbers of units for
estimating M and M^f is generally outweighed by the disadvantage of not
pairing. How much the pairing reduces the variance of $\hat{C}$ depends on g, on
the correlation between paired sampling units, and on the herbage mass
estimates.

Whether in system 1 the cages should be placed near other units depends
on the correlations between the estimates concerned. Usually the size and
shape of the cage units is not equal to the size and shape of the other units.
This reduces the correlation between $\hat{M}^{f,e}$ and $\hat{M}$ and causes the variance of
the cage units to be different from the variance of other units, making a

different number of cage units compared with other units advantageous. It is generally advisable therefore not to group the 3 types of units. Because g is less than 1 and the standard error of $\hat{M}^f$ usually is not much smaller than the standard error of $\hat{M}$, in system 2 the total number of sampling units required is reduced when choosing relatively more pairs of sampling units in the pasture than in the exclosure.

The choice between systems 1 and 2 is often not obvious. When the shape of the cages is quite different from the shape of the other sampling units, system 2 will probably be more precise when using the same number of units on both systems, but there may be other situations in which system 1 is more precise. The choice between these systems is not a matter of precision alone. The cost and labour requirements may be larger when cages are used, and the importance of possible systematic errors must be considered. The possible bias caused by measuring the accumulation on a separate part of the pasture in system 2 has to be balanced against the possible disturbance caused by the cages in the pasture using system 1.

2.4.3   Precision of herbage intake measurements

2.4.3.1 *Sward-cutting techniques.* Some results on the precision of estimating herbage intake in grazing experiments have been summarised by Meijs (1981). Some recent results from homogeneous temperate swards are reported in Table 2.5. The preceding management of all the swards involved cutting. The size and shape of the sampling units (strips) have been described in Table 2.3, pre- and post-grazing strips were paired, and the grazing period was 3-4 days. The herbage accumulation during grazing was measured on a separate area of the pasture, and the equation of Linehan was used for the estimation of the intake. Due to the low accumulation rate Walters and Evans (1979) made no correction for accumulation in their results.

The standard error from the systematic sample of Meijs (1981) was calculated as if it was a simple random sample which may have over-estimated the standard error of intake. The experimental conditions from which the data in Table 2.5 were derived were optimal for the sward-cutting method (short grazing periods, pairing of pre- and post-grazing sample sites, clean pastures, homogeneous swards). In many experimental conditions such as in native range or tropical pastures, sampling intensity has to be higher if the same precision as that reported in Table 2.5 is to be achieved.

2.4.3.2 *Non-destructive techniques.* No critical studies have been carried out to investigate the comparative precision of non-destructive sward sampling techniques when used to assess herbage intake. However, results of many

Table 2.5   Characteristics of the sampling procedure for the estimation of the herbage mass at the start and at the end of the grazing period and of the intake.

Reference	Meijs (1981)			Walters and Evans (1979)		
Cutting equipment	Motorscythe + lawnmower			Sheep-shearing head		
Animals	Lactating cows			Sheep		
Type of sward	Permanent sward, 80-90% perennial ryegrass			Monoculture Perennial ryegrass or cocksfoot		
Type of sampling	Systematic			Stratified random		
Number of pairs	1	3	10	1	3	10
M		2596			2687	
$\sigma_{\hat{M}}$	180	104	57	242	140	77
ρ_1		0.7			—	
M^f		1366			1263	
$\sigma_{\hat{M}^f}$	174	100	55	172	99	54
ρ_2		0.5			0.5	
C		1489			1423	
$\sigma_{\hat{C}}$	261	151	83	279	161	88
I		113.7			65.3	
$\sigma_{\hat{I}}$	20.0	11.5	6.3	12.8	7.4	4.0
$^{CV}\hat{C} = {}^{CV}\hat{I}$	17.6	10.1	5.6	19.6	11.3	6.2

M   = herbage mass at the start of a grazing period (kg ha^{-1})
M^f = residual herbage at the end of a grazing period (kg ha^{-1})
σ   = standard error of the estimate
ρ_1 = correlation between the herbage masses at two adjacent sampling units at the start of the grazing period
ρ_2 = correlation between the herbage mass of two adjacent sampling units, one at the start and the other at the end of the grazing period
C   = herbage consumed (kg ha^{-1})
I   = consumption of herbage (g day^{-1}/kg$^{0.75}$)
CV   = coefficient of variation of the estimate

All data are expressed in organic matter.

studies have been published on their value for estimating herbage mass. The following general points emerge:
1) All non-destructive techniques are less precise than cutting methods on a per sample basis, they therefore require a greater intensity of sampling to achieve an equivalent level of precision.
2) The methods based on capacitance tend to be less precise than height measurement (ie disc meter) which in turn, tends to be less than visual appraisal.

3) Relative precision is less for post-grazed swards than for pre-grazed swards.

4) The adoption of a system of stratified random sampling improves precision.

5) Variability of pastures in terms of botanical composition, sward structure, morphology, sward density and moisture content decreases precision — particularly for the capacitance method.

For improved temperate pastures, calibration curves should be based on 5-9 points, and subsequent random pasture measurements should be made at an intensity of 30-75 per ha in order to give coefficients of variation of around 10% for estimates of herbage mass. Under more variable pasture conditions, such as native hill, range, or tropical pastures, the necessary sampling intensity can be expected to be higher. In all cases it is recommended that workers should conduct preliminary studies on the errors associated with the particular pastures and conditions they are studying before adopting a sampling procedure. When using these techniques the possibility of bias must always be considered and frequent calibrations should be made.

2.5   DIET SELECTION

It is often necessary in grazing trials to obtain information on the nutritive quality and botanical composition of herbage ingested by the grazing animal. Due to selection by the animal this will often differ from that of the herbage on offer and some attempt to assess dietary composition other than that based on herbage on offer is essential if relative differences between pastures in terms of animal production are to be interpreted critically.

2.5.1   Assessing the quality of grazed herbage

Two types of sward sampling methods are used:

1) Samples which represent the herbage grazed by the animals are obtained by cutting at "grazing height" or by hand plucking. These samples are chemically analysed and the results are assumed to relate closely to the composition of the herbage eaten. The intensity of sampling depends on the heterogeneity of the pasture. For temperate improved pastures 8-20 samples per ha have been recommended (eg Brown, 1954). Samples are obtained immediately before or during grazing and one should attempt to sample vegetation that is typical of that being grazed. One method is to match the sample for analysis with that removed by the grazing animal after inspection of samples obtained before and after grazing (Cook, 1964; Kalmbacher and Washko, 1977).

The above method is clearly subjective and liable to unknown bias. For example Langlands (1974) found that hand plucking overestimated digestibility and N content in high quality pastures, and underestimated these components in low quality pastures when compared with samples obtained from oesophageal fistulated sheep. However, where within-pasture variability in quality is very marked, as in some range and tropical pastures, the above method can provide more useful guidance to dietary composition than that based on samples taken by cutting at an arbitrary height.

2) Nutrient composition of grazed herbage is obtained indirectly by "difference". Samples cut before and after grazing to provide herbage mass data are used to provide sub-samples for chemical analysis or for determination of *in-vitro* digestibility. The quantity of each nutrient removed during grazing is calculated and expressed as a percentage of the OM removed as follows:

$$X = \frac{Y - Y^f}{M - M^f} \cdot 100 \tag{2.8}$$

where X = concentration of nutrient in herbage grazed; Y = kg ha^{-1} of nutrient before grazing; Y^f = kg ha^{-1} of nutrient after grazing; M = kg ha^{-1} of organic matter before grazing; M^f = kg ha^{-1} of organic matter after grazing.

This method involves the chemical analysis of two sets of samples as well as sampling for herbage mass before and after grazing, consequently the errors associated with the qualitative estimates of grazed herbage are the results of accumulated error for estimates of the four components on the right hand side of the above equation.

Provided that care is taken to obtain valid data for mass, and samples are uncontaminated by soil and faeces, reasonably accurate data can be obtained. For example, Walters & Evans (1979) found that the coefficients of variation of estimates of digestibility of herbage grazed were only marginally higher by this method than by indirect animal techniques, and comparative digestibility estimates were in good agreement with those based on faecal nitrogen/digestibility regressions obtained in indoor feeding trials.

2.5.2 Assessing the botanical composition of grazed herbage

Sward sampling methods designed to assess the botanical composition of herbage grazed are similar in principle to those described for nutritive quality assessment. Thus two basic techniques can be identified:

(1) Identifying and quantifying botanical components in samples purporting to represent grazed herbage. This technique, like that for quality assessment is subjective and liable to unknown bias. It cannot be recommended for many critical research studies, but can provide better guidance under some range or tropical conditions than indiscriminate sampling by cutting.

(2) Identifying and quantifying by "difference" the botanical components removed by the grazing animal from samples cut to provide data on herbage mass before and after grazing.

In both cases the techniques require that botanical components be expressed on a weight basis. Samples are analysed for botanical composition either directly by manual separation or by indirect methods as reviewed by Brown (1954) and 't Mannetje (1978).

2.6 REFERENCES

ALDER, F E and MINSON, D J (1963). The herbage intake of cattle grazing lucerne and cocksfoot pastures *Journal of Agricultural Science, Cambridge,*60, 359-369.

ANGELONE, A. TOLEDO, J M and BURNS, J C (1980a). Herbage measurement *in situ* by electronics. 1. The multiple proe type capacitance meter: a brief review. *Grass and Forage Science,* 35, 25-33.

ANGELONE, A, TOLEDO, J M and BURNS, J C (1980b). Herbage measurement *in situ* by electronics. 2. Theory and design of an earth plate capacitance meter for estimating forage dry matter. *Grass and Forage Science,* 35, 95-103.

BAKHUIS, J A (1960). Estimating pasture production by use of grass length and sward density. *Netherlands Journal of Agricultural Science,* 8, 211-224.

BOSCH, S (1956). The determination of pasture yield. *Netherlands Journal of Agricultural Science,* 4, 305-313.

BROWN, DOROTHY (1954). Methods of surveying and measuring vegetation. *Bulletin Commonwealth Bureau of Pastures and Field Crops, Hurley, Berkshire, England,* No 42, 223 pp.

C.A.B. (1961). Research techniques in use at the Grassland Research Institute, Hurley. *Bulletin Commonwealth Bureau of Pastures and Field Crops, Hurley, Berkshire, England,* No 45, 166 pp.

CARTER, J F (1962). Herbage sampling for yield: tame pastures. In: Pasture and range research techniques. American Society of Agronomy and others (eds). *Comstock Publishing Associates, Ithaca, USA.*

COCHRAN, W G (1969). Sampling techniques. *John Wiley & Sons, New York.*

COOK, C W (1964). Symposium on nutrition of forages and pastures. Collecting forage samples representative of ingested material of grazing animals for nutritional studies. *Journal of Animal Science,* 23, 265-270.

EARLE, D F and McGOWAN, A A (1979). Evaluation and calibration of an automated rising plate meter for estimating dry matter yield of pasture. *Australian Journal of Experimental Agriculture and Animal Husbandry,* 19, 337-343.

FRAME, J (1981). Herbage mass. In: J Hodgson, R D Baker, Alison Davies, A S Laidlaw, J D Leaver (eds) *Sward Measurement Handbook,* pp. 39-69. The British Grassland Society.

HARDY, A, PHILIPPEAU, G and TRENCHEFORT, J (1978). L'estimation de la production d'herbe d'une prairie. *Perspectives agricoles,* 14, 36.

HAYDOCK, K P and SHAW, N H (1975). The comparative yield method for estimating dry matter yield of pasture. *Australian Journal of Experimental Agriculture and Animal Husbandry,* 15, 663-670.

HUTCHINSON, K J, MCLEAN, R W and HAMILTON, B A (1972). The visual estimation of pasture availability using standard pasture cores. *Journal of the British Grassland Society,* 27, 29-34.

JONES, R J and HAYDOCK, K P (1970). Yield estimation of tropical and temperate pasture species using an electronic pasture meter. *Journal of Agricultural Science, Cambridge,* 75, 27-36.

KALMBACHER, R S and WASHKO, J B (1977). Time magnitude and quality estimates of forage consumed by deer in woodland clearways. *Agronomy Journal,* 69, 497.

LANGLANDS, J P (1974). Studies on the nutritive value of the diet selected by grazing sheep. VII. A note on hand plucking as a technique for estimating dietary composition. *Animal Production*, 19, 249-252.

LINEHAN, P A, LOWE, J and STEWART, R H (1947). The output of pasture and its measurement. Part II. *Journal of the British Grassland Society*, 2, 145-168.

MATCHES, A G (1963). A cordless hedge trimmer for herbage Sampling. *Agronomy Journal*, 55, 309.

MEIJS, J A C (1981). Herbage intake by grazing dairy cows. Agricultural Research Report 909. *Centre for Agricultural Publishing and Documentation, Wageningen, The Netherlands.*

McINTYRE, G A (1978). Statistical aspects of vegetation sampling. In: Mannetje, L 't (ed). Measurement of grassland vegetation and animal production. *Bulletin Commonwealth Agricultural Bureaux, Hurley, Berkshire, England,* No 52, pp 8-21.

NEAL, D L and NEAL, J L (1973). Uses and capabilities of electronic capacitance instruments for estimating standing herbage, Part 1. History and Development. *Journal of the British Grassland Society*, 28, 81-89.

NOMOTO , T (1975). New type of grassmeter for pasture yield estimation. *Japanese Agricultural Research Quarterly*, 9,165.

PECHANEC, J P and PICKFORD, G D (1937). A weight estimate method for the determination of range or pasture production. *Journal of the American Society of Agronomy*, 29, 894-904.

't MANNETJE, L (1978). Measuring quantity of grassland vegetation. In: Mannetje, L 't (ed). Measurement of Grassland Vegetation and Animal Production. *Bulletin Commonwealth Agricultural Bureaux, Hurley, Berkshire, England,* No 52, pp 63-95.

WALTERS, R J K and EVANS, E M (1979). Evaluation of a sward sampling technique for estimating herbage intake by grazing sheep. *Grass and Forage Science*, 34, 37-44.

CHAPTER 3

ANIMAL BASED TECHNIQUES FOR ESTIMATING HERBAGE INTAKE

Y.L.P. Le Du and P.D. Penning

3.1 INTRODUCTION

Estimating the feed intake of a grazing animal must by definition rely upon techniques imposing minimal disturbance to the normal grazing activity of that animal. The sward cutting methods described in Chapter 2 impose little interference on the animal *per se*, but their application is limited to specific grazing situations and they can only provide an estimate of the mean intake of a group. The animal-based techniques, whilst of necessity requiring some interference with the grazing livestock, are potentially usable in a wide range of grazing circumstances and allow some examination of between-animal variation. Three basic techniques have been used and these are, a) faeces output/diet digestibility, b) weighing animals, and c) water turnover. All three techniques are described but because of their greater importance, most of this chapter is concerned with the methods for estimating faeces production and digestibility of the diet selected by the grazing animal.

3.2 FAECAL OUTPUT AND DIET DIGESTIBILITY

The expression used to calculate intake from estimates of faecal output and diet digestibility is obtained from a simple manipulation of the digestibility relationship:

$$\text{Digestibility (D)} = \frac{\text{Intake (I)} - \text{Faecal output (F)}}{\text{Intake (I)}} \qquad (3.1)$$

or

$$I = \frac{F}{(1 - D)}$$

Measurement of I is therefore dependent upon accurate estimation of F and D. It should be noted that error in estimation of F leads to equivalent error in I but that error in D, since D is generally greater than 0.50, leads to a proportionately larger error in $(1 - D)$ and consequently in intake.

Methods of estimating F and D are described in the following two sections.

3.3   FAECAL OUTPUT
3.3.1   **Total collection**

Total faeces output can be measured by harnessing animals and fitting dung bags to collect all the faeces voided. The advantage of this total collection method is that it is relatively simple and very few laboratory facilities are required. If dung is to be collected from female animals, urine separators may have to be used, particularly with cattle, to prevent urine contaminating the faeces. With female sheep it is possible to use mesh bags, provided the faeces produced are relatively dry and pelleted.

Harnesses, dung bags and separators should be fitted to the animal several days before a collection period. This acclimatisation also allows adjustments to be made to ensure that the harnesses fit properly and that faeces are not lost from the bags.

The number of days over which a faeces collection is made will vary according to experimental conditions. It is recommended that faeces should be collected over a minimum of five days, this being a compromise between the minimum length of time required to give a reasonable estimate of faeces production and to reflect changes that may be occurring in the digestibility and composition of the herbage being eaten. Continuous collection of faeces will give the best estimate of production but this is not usually practical.

3.3.1.1 *Equipment*. There are numerous designs for harnesses and dung bags. However, no specific types of harness appear to have outstanding advantages. Detailed descriptions of harness are given by Lesperance and Bohman (1961), Royal (1968), Cammell (1977) and Michell (1977).

3.3.1.2 *Sampling of faeces*. The frequency with which dung bags should be emptied is determined by the volume of fresh faeces produced. Twice daily is generally recommended but once daily may be sufficient when intake is very low, whilst three or four times daily may be necessary for dairy cows producing large volumes of faeces.

Generally it is necessary to sub-sample the faeces daily owing to the quantities voided; after weighing and mixing thoroughly an aliquot sample is taken and these are then bulked over the measurement period. Sub-sampling may not be necessary where intake is very low or the animals are very young and are eating little solid food.

3.3.1.3 *Processing of faeces samples*. The aliquot samples of faeces may be dried daily in a forced draught oven at 100°C and the dried samples bulked, mixed and sub-sampled again at the end of the experimental period. Alternatively, the samples can be frozen and stored until the end of the collection period. They are then allowed to thaw, thoroughly mixed and, if necessary, sub-samples taken for drying prior to chemical analysis.

For drying, the faeces samples are placed in a solid-bottomed tray and dried at 100°C for 48 hours. Drying faeces at 100°C is not recommended if chemical analyses for various fibre fractions (with the exception of modified acid detergent fibre) are to be subsequently performed. If faeces are to be sampled for neutral detergent fibre (NDF), acid detergent fibre (ADF) and lignin, samples should be freeze dried; nitrogen (N) analyses should be carried out on undried faeces where possible. After drying, the faeces are milled and stored in sealed bags until analysed.

3.3.1.4 *Disadvantages of total collection*. The disadvantages of total collection of faeces are:
- i)   Weighing and sub-sampling large quantities of faeces requires relatively high labour inputs. Approximate labour requirements

are one person for twelve cows or fifty sheep (solely to look after harnesses, change dung bags and weigh, dry and sample faeces).
ii)   The animal's behaviour and performance may be affected if poorly-designed harnesses are used.
iii)   Collection from female animals is more difficult as it normally requires the separation of faeces from urine.
iv)   Faeces may be lost from the bags, giving under-estimates of production.
v)   Herbage production and animal performance may be affected by the prevention of the return of faeces to the pasture.

3.3.2. Estimation of faeces production using markers (indicators)

The criteria for the ideal marker to estimate faeces production were listed by Raymond and Minson (1955) as follows:
i)   It should be quantitatively recovered in the faeces (ie neither absorbed nor abnormally retained in the digestive tract).
ii)   It should be non-toxic.
iii)   It should be readily analysed by physical or chemical methods.
iv)   It should be present only in small amounts in the original diet.

Using a marker, faeces production can be estimated from the following equation:

$$\text{Daily faeces produced (g)} = \frac{\text{Weight of marker given (g day}^{-1}) \qquad \text{x RR}}{\text{Mean concentration of marker in faeces (g g}^{-1})} \qquad (3.2)$$

RR is the recovery rate of the marker and is:

$$\frac{\text{Total weight of marker excreted in faeces (g)}}{\text{Total weight of marker given (g)}} \qquad (3.3)$$

RR is generally not measured within an experiment and is assumed to be 1.

Currently the most widely used marker is chromic oxide (Cr_2O_3). This marker was first suggested by Edin (1918) and its use has been described in detail in a review of the use of markers in nutrition by Kotb and Luckey (1972).

3.3.2.1 *Carriers for the marker.* Numerous types of carriers for Cr_2O_3 have been tried but only three are in general use:
i)   Commercially produced gelatine capsules containing 1 g or 10 g

    Cr_2O_3 in an oil base (manufactured by R P Scherer, Bath Road, Slough, Berks).

ii)   Paper impregnated with Cr_2O_3 (contact authors for suppliers).

iii)   Where animals are individually fed known quantities of a feed (usually concentrates) it is possible to incorporate the marker into this feed.

    Corbett *et al* (1958; 1959) found that the flow of Cr_2O_3 through the duodenum was more regular when it was administered in impregnated paper than in gelatine capsules. However, using paper impregnated with Cr_2O_3 has one major disadvantage; doses have to be weighed individually and then packaged. Methods of preparation have been described by Troelsen (1963; 1966) and Moran and Gomez (1977).

    Foliar application of chromic oxide was investigated by Harris *et al* (1967). However, although the marker appeared to be uniformly distributed, its concentration was too low to be used as an indicator.

    Watson and Laby (1978) reported the use of a continuous dosing system using ^{51}Cr-EDTA. Syringes containing the marker were placed into the rumen and automatically released the marker over several weeks. Laby (personal communication) has suggested that Cr_2O_3 could be administered in this manner. This method has not yet been tried but if successful would greatly reduce labour requirements and tend to reduce some of the biases found with other methods of dosing.

3.3.2.2   *Dosing and sampling frequencies.* Concentration of Cr_2O_3 in the faeces may show considerable diurnal fluctuations when it is administered in discrete doses. For example, Hardison and Reid (1953) found a variation in recovery rate from 0.55 at 12.00 hours to 1.8 at 18.00 hours for steers kept indoors and for grazing steers the variation was from 0.8 to 1.3. All animals were dosed once daily with 10g Cr_2O_3 and the animals kept indoors were fed twice daily (at 06.00 hours and 16.00 hours) while the grazing animals ingested most of their feed between 18.00 hours and 08.00 hours. The substances used as carriers for the Cr_2O_3 and the patterns of dosing and sampling of the animals should be designed to minimise or take into account these fluctuations in Cr_2O_3 excretion.

    A preliminary dosing period is necessary to ensure stable conditions are reached prior to sampling the faeces to determine marker concentration. The time required for Cr_2O_3 to equilibrate throughout the gut is influenced by the level of intake and by the characteristics of the feed, as the rate of excretion of the marker is related to the rate of passage through the digestive tract. Various periods for preliminary dosing have been used for an equilibrium to be reached but in practice a minimum period of seven days is recommended.

Faeces samples should be taken at times when the concentration of the marker is similar to the mean daily value. Normally animals are brought into pens and faeces samples are taken from the rectum (grab sampling). Lambourne (1957) concluded that an unbiased estimate of the mean marker concentration was obtained by dosing the animals and taking samples of faeces at 9 and 15 hour intervals. Coop and Hill (1962), using this dosing and faeces sampling pattern, confirmed that marker concentration was within 1% of the mean concentration, although faeces samples taken at 2 hour intervals showed a diurnal variation of ± 12% from the mean.

More frequent administration of the marker appears to eliminate diurnal variation of marker concentration in the faeces. Pigden and Brisson (1956) and Brisson *et al* (1957) claimed that no variation in Cr_2O_3 concentration occurred in the faeces of grazing animals when the marker was administered in gelatine capsules every four hours. However, this frequency of dosing is not usually practical.

Raymond and Minson (1955) outlined a method of faeces sampling where faeces are collected from a number of rings each of 8.4 m^2 distributed at random over the sward. Because of the random nature of this technique the bias introduced by taking faeces samples at fixed times is considerably reduced. However, differences in climatic conditions, insect populations, wild animals, etc, could introduce important errors with this technique. A modification of this method was applied by Minson *et al* (1960) who identified the individual defaecations of cattle by dosing the animals with coloured polystyrene granules. However, this method did not prove successful with sheep. The method of Raymond and Minson (1955) is suitable where the intake of a group of animals is required but individual sampling is recommended when estimating the intake of individuals.

3.3.2.3 *Chemical determination of chromic oxide.* Several methods for digesting and analysing Cr_2O_3 have been described in the literature. The digestion procedure was outlined by Stevenson and De Langen (1960) and a method for the analysis of chromium by continuous flow automatic colorimetry was given by Stevenson and Clare (1963). Williams *et al* (1962) described a method for estimating chromium by atomic absorption spectrophotometry. Full details of the method used at the Grassland Research Institute are given in 3.9.1.

When deciding on the dose rate of Cr_2O_3 required it is desirable to aim for a minimum concentration of 5 mg g^{-1} faeces DM to facilitate chemical determination. However, concentrations as low as 0.5 mg g^{-1} faeces DM can be accurately determined using atomic absorption.

3.3.2.4 *Methods of minimising error and bias.* When Cr_2O_3 is used to estimate faeces production, the technique is normally not checked within every experiment. However, when using this technique for the first time and periodically thereafter, it is advisable to carry out some or all of the checks listed below:

i) Where possible some animals on the experimental treatments should be fitted with harnesses and dung bags and the recovery rate of Cr_2O_3 checked. Faeces production can then be adjusted, if necessary, for recovery rate.

ii) Some animals should not be dosed with Cr_2O_3 and their faeces sampled for the marker, (this applies particularly where pastures are continuously stocked and Cr_2O_3 is administered over long periods). Cr_2O_3 recovery rate should then be adjusted for any measurable marker found in the control animals.

iii) Some losses of Cr_2O_3 may occur in the preparation (particularly grinding of the samples) for chemical analysis (Stevenson 1962). Known quantities of Cr_2O_3 should be added to faeces and its quantitative recovery checked.

iv) In commercial grades of Cr_2O_3 there may be contamination with small amounts of soluble dichromates and therefore the material used should be checked for solubility.

3.3.2.5 *Accuracy of faeces output measurements.* The total collection of faeces from animals fitted with harnesses and dung bags gives an unbiased estimate of total faeces produced provided none are lost. In certain circumstances however total collection may not be practical.

Streeter (1969) and Theurer (1970) have considered in detail advantages and disadvantages of different methods to estimate faeces production and these will not be considered further. However, faeces estimation using markers becomes inaccurate when the mean retention time of a marker changes appreciably just prior to or during faeces collection. If the mean retention time of the marker is increased, less marker will be excreted and faeces production will be over-estimated. This can happen for example, if herbage availability or digestibility is changed suddenly during this period. Under these circumstances total collection must be made.

Langlands *et al* (1963a,b) reported that the mean coefficient of variation (CV) for the rate of recovery for Cr_2O_3, given in impregnated paper, was 7.2% and for Cr_2O_3 given in capsules was 9.4% for 3 day sampling periods. They found that for periods of t days (t > 3), then the CV is given by $7.2 \sqrt{\frac{3}{t}}$ for paper and $9.4 \sqrt{\frac{3}{t}}$ for capsules. Valderrabano (1979) found that there was little difference between Cr_2O_3 capsules and Cr_2O_3 given in paper. He found a CV of 9.0% between animals (sheep) for Cr_2O_3 recovery and a CV of 3% between treatments.

The authors found the mean recovery rate for Cr_2O_3 from 55 experiments reported in the literature to be 96.5% (SD $\pm$ 5.6%). These experiments included cattle and sheep, different types of feed, carriers for Cr_2O_3, preliminary dosing periods and frequencies of dosing and sampling. Calculations from data in the literature were also made of the total faeces production estimates by Cr_2O_3 concentration compared with measured faeces production; the mean figure found was 96.1% (SD $\pm$6.2).

It is therefore concluded that using Cr_2O_3 as a marker will generally estimate faeces output to within $\pm$ 6%. The following procedures are recommended: A preliminary dosing period of 7 days with animals being dosed twice daily at approximately 8 and 16 hour intervals and faeces samples taken at the same time over at least a 5 day period. Use of Cr_2O_3 in a slow release form, ie paper, reduces diurnal variation in marker excretion and slightly improves the accuracy of estimation.

3.3.2.6 *Other markers.* Several elements of the rare earth elements, inert metals and radio-active nuclides have been used as faecal markers. Included in this group are Eu, Dy, Au; and [144]Ce, [46]Sc, [95]Zr, [140]La, [91]Y, [106]Ru; and [198]Au.

Other radio-active markers that have been used include ^{51}Cr-EDTA, [51]Cr_2O_3 and [131]Ba SO_4. Cr_2O_3, Ti O_2, Cr-EDTA, Ba SO_4, CuSCn and ruthenium tris (1,10 phenanthraline) chloride (Ru complex) (Tan *et al*, 1971) have also been used. However, of these markers only two, in addition to Cr_2O_3, appear to have been used on any scale; these are Cr-EDTA and the Ru complex.

Morgan *et al* (1976) have compared dosing with Cr_2O_3 and constant infusions of Ru complex or Cr-EDTA. They concluded that small portable pumps could be fitted to the animals for infusing the two soluble markers and that Cr-EDTA had advantages over either Cr_2O_3 or the Ru complex. Where a constant rate of infusion of Cr-EDTA was achieved they found that faeces could be sampled once daily and the period of measurement could be reduced. Another advantage of the Cr-EDTA technique was the ease of sample analysis for chromium; 100 g samples of faeces, together with 270 g water and 10 ml HC1 were macerated in a blender, left overnight and then centrifuged. Chromium concentration was then determined in the supernatant by atomic absorption. The authors concluded that this analysis requires less than 10% of the time taken to analyse Cr_2O_3. However, these workers do not appear to have taken account of losses of Cr-EDTA in the urine. At present it can be concluded that $Cr_2O_3$is the most suitable marker.

3.4 DIET DIGESTIBILITY

Digestibility cannot be measured directly *in vivo* in the grazing animal and therefore a number of indirect methods have been developed. Major amongst these are the ratio technique, the faecal index technique and the *in vitro* digestibility procedures; the potential of each of these is examined below.

3.4.1 The ratio technique

The digestibility of herbage can be accurately estimated from the ratio of the concentration of an indigestible plant component in the feed to that of the component in the faeces:

$$\text{Herbage intake (I)} \times i_h = \text{Faeces output (F)} \times i_f \qquad (3.4)$$

(where i_h and i_f are percentages of a component in feed and faeces respectively).

$$\text{Therefore the digestibility coefficient} = 1 - \frac{i_h}{i_f} \qquad (3.5)$$

This technique requires (i) that the marker be unaltered in its passage through the animal, (ii) that it be quantitatively recoverable, and (iii) that feed and faeces be accurately sampled.

The major plant components that have been suggested as potential markers are lignin, chromogen and silica. Although all have been widely used in the past, serious doubts are now cast on their suitability for a number of reasons. For example, neither lignin nor chromogen are specific entities and the recoveries of both are influenced by sample treatment. In all cases the contents of marker can be highly variable between plant species, parts of individual plants, growth stages and times of harvest. Equally, the accuracy of analytical procedures for determining the very low concentration of these indicators in both feed and faeces is not good. However, where the proportion of indicator in the plant is high, for example lignin in mature tropical forages, this technique may work reasonably well.

With the development of new and improved analytical procedures, silica offers the best potential for the future but at this stage the ratio technique cannot be recommended for routine use.

3.4.2 The faecal index technique

This method requires a conventional indoor *in vivo* digestibility trial to be undertaken with herbage similar to that being grazed, and that a faecal component is related to *in vivo* digestibility; this component need not be indigestible. The concentration of this component is then assessed in faecal samples from the grazing animals (making allowance for any diurnal pattern in its excretion) and the diet digestibility predicted from the relationship derived indoors. If the faecal concentration of the component selected is positively related to digestibility, the error caused by differences in level of intake between the grazing and digestibility trial animals is minimised (Langlands and Bennett, 1973).

Nitrogen is the faecal component most frequently used and the technique is at its best when local regressions are produced for each specific set of circumstances, since the between herbage factors are the major source of variation in the parameters of the regression. Harvesting of herbage, for the initial *in vivo* digestibility trial which is representative of the herbage consumed by the free-grazing animals is the major difficulty. A digestibility trial running in parallel with the grazing experiment is required with its attendant labour and facility requirements. In many cases sheep have been used in the digestibility trials, to minimise the work load, and the regressions applied to grazing cattle. This method is questionable since differences in efficiency of digestion between species have been reported (Blaxter *et al*, 1966; Playne, 1978). The usefulness is therefore restricted to situations in which herbage equivalent to that being grazed can be harvested for a contemporary digestibility trial undertaken with the same class of animal as that in the main grazing experiment. One major advantage is that the attendant analytical requirements are simple.

To minimise error in the estimation of the digestibility of grazed pasture the N regression "must be derived with material similar to that selected by the animal when grazing" (Langlands, 1967 b) since general relationships have been shown to be imprecise as a result of effects of season and fertilizer treatment on the relationship between faecal N and digestibility. For example, Raymond *et al* (1954) and Minson and Kemp (1961) demonstrated residual standard deviations of $\pm$ 5.7 and $\pm$ 4.0 digestibility units respectively for general relationships. The fulfilment of Langlands' pre-requisite limits the range of grazing management conditions in which the technique can be applied. Firstly, the sward must be tall enough to mow; secondly, if herbage availability is high and/or heterogeneous in composition the grazers may, for example, select disproportionately more of one species than another or of leaf than of stem so that the relationship of digestibility to N percentage differs from that obtained with cut herbage.

This technique is therefore of little use under continuous grazing management or in swards where opportunities exist for widespread selection between plants or parts of plants. It is at its best under a strip-grazing management in which the herbage removed by the grazing animal is equivalent to that harvested by machine for the indoor digestibility trial. Deviation from this condition will increase the likelihood of error or bias in the estimate of digestibility.

3.4.2.1 *Derivation of a nitrogen regression.* To derive an N regression it is necessary to run a standard digestibility trial (Schneider and Flatt, 1975) feeding fresh grass similar to that offered to the grazing animals whose intakes are to be estimated. The measurements required are: feed intake and faecal output (DM), ash content of feed and faeces and faecal N percentage.

Greenhalgh *et al* (1960) demonstrated that using three animals and sub-periods of three days the standard error of prediction need not be greater than 1.0 unit of digestibility; this may be slightly reduced if longer periods are used. However, if the digestibility of the grass being fed is changing with time, sub-periods should be kept as short as practical.

The animals used in the digestibility trial must be housed individually, equipped with faecal collection equipment and offered herbage at a level of intake as close as possible to that anticipated for their grazing contemporaries. The animals should be introduced to their digestibility stalls and offered fresh grass for at least one week prior to the commencement of the trial to allow acclimatization to the feed, the surroundings and the equipment. This is of particular importance for inexperienced animals and it also permits their potential intake indoors to be estimated. Once this has been established the level of feeding for the trial can be set, since it is essential that the animals consume all the grass offered each day and are not able to preferentially select. The level of intake set for the trial should be no more than 90% of *ad libitum* if total consumption is to be achieved.

Every effort should be made to minimise deterioration of the herbage between cutting and eating. It should be offered in at least two feeds per day and as many as five may be necessary when high levels of intake are achieved, for example with dairy cows fed highly digestible herbage. The weather conditions will also influence the feeding and indeed the cutting frequency necessary; in hot and/or humid conditions it may be necessary to cut the herbage twice daily or to cold store it to minimise heating of the material (see Chapter 5).

The established level of herbage intake should be maintained for at least four days prior to the commencement of faecal collection in order to equilibrate faecal output and the concentration of N therein. A standard quantity of grass dry matter should be fed daily. Some method of rapid assessment of dry matter content in the fresh material must therefore be employed since the first feed of grass is offered as soon as possible after cutting. The precise output of faeces attributable to any given feed is impossible to define but, because of gut residence time, some lag of faecal collection behind feeding can be introduced. If the previously stated introductory periods are maintained, a lag of faecal collection behind feed intake of between 24 and 48 hours would seem appropriate.

Depending upon the class of animal, level of intake and faecal collection equipment used, faeces will need to be removed from the collection bag or tray from 1-3 times daily; at least one of these must coincide with the offering of a new day's feed (eg at 10.00 hours) so that intake and output can be equated. At each collection the total weight of fresh faeces is recorded and two samples are taken. The first is dried to permit calculation of the faecal dry matter output, whilst the second is taken for bulking with all other aliquots for that period. After sampling, these latter portions should be frozen and cold stored. At the end of each period they are thawed and mixed thoroughly prior to sampling for chemical analyses for dry matter, ash and N contents. The N analysis should preferably be undertaken on fresh material since drying can radically affect N content. If this is not possible then faeces samples from both digestibility and grazing trials must be dried in the same manner and their N content determined on the dry material.

The N regression from the digestibility trial is then derived as N % of faeces (x) against *in vivo* digestibility (Y).

By inverse interpolation this regression equation can be used to estimate the digestibility of the diet selected by the grazing animals from the N content of their faeces. The calculations are best undertaken on an ash-free or organic matter basis since this permits elimination of any effects due to soil contamination. A polynomial form should be fitted to the data since in some cases a linear model does not provide the best fit (eg Greenhalgh and Corbett, 1960). When applying such an equation to grazing animals, faeces samples are taken from each individual. These can be from the total faeces or from grab samples. In the latter it may be necessary to correct for diurnal variation in the percentage of N but it is generally considered that faecal N content varies little through the day, unlike that of external markers.

Grazing animals generally have a higher intake than animals fed indoors (Minson and Raymond, 1958). These workers reported a decrease of about 1.5 percentage units in OM digestibility when forage intake was increased by 50%, although when digestibility was estimated by faecal N concentration in the faeces the predicted decrease in digestibility was only 0.66 units. Similarly, Valderrabano (1979) reported that when intake was increased from maintenance to twice maintenance, digestibility fell by 3 units, but the fall in digestibility predicted from an N regression was 0.7 units. Therefore, N regression may over-estimate the digestibility of diets selected by grazing animals if based upon animals with a-markedly lower intake than those grazing.

3.4.2.2 *Cutting and preparing the forage.* When harvesting forage for a digestibility trial, consideration must be given to obtaining material as similar to that grazed as possible. In particular, height of cut must be carefully considered since this can have a major influence on the proportions of leaf and stem, and live and dead material in the harvested herbage. The aim should be to use a machine that does minimum physical damage to the crop, to reduce problems of rejection caused by physical damage and heating, the latter resulting from bacterial action during the period prior to consumption. For sheep trials it is possible to use two-wheeled reciprocating knife mowers (Penning and Gibb, 1979) and then to collect the grass by hand. With cattle this is impractical and some form of mechanical harvesting is necessary. A drum mower followed by a forage wagon fitted with a pick-up reel may provide the best combination for this purpose and does minimal damage to the crop. A one pass operation with a forage harvester results in laceration of the herbage which can subsequently lead to very rapid heating of the material, although this can be overcome by the use of a silage additive such as formic acid; indeed, higher intakes of zero-grazed herbage treated with an additive as opposed to untreated material have been reported (Anon 1977) and were attributed solely to the reduction in heating of the material.

Once the herbage has been harvested a representative sample must be taken, and a dry matter estimation made if the rations are to be offered on a predetermined dry weight basis. This can best be accomplished using either a microwave drying technique (Schild and Honig, 1975) or by heating in oil (Brown and Duval, 1907; Cammell, 1977). An alternative that may be used if these rapid drying techniques are unavailable is for an experienced worker to estimate the dry matter content of the grass, offer half of the total dry matter on the basis of this estimate, then dry a sample overnight in an oven at 100°C, correcting any errors in the estimate with this figure, prior to feeding the remainder of the 24 hour allocation the following morning.

3.4.3   The *in vitro* digestibility procedures

A number of laboratory procedures have been developed for the prediction of *in vitro* digestibility. Two methods are pre-eminent in their accuracy and precision; these are the *in vitro* procedures using rumen liquor (Tilley and Terry, 1963) and the cellulose solubility technique (Jones and Hayward, 1975). These are the preferred laboratory methods with the *in vitro* being the better, particularly where a range of forage species samples is being examined (Terry *et al*, 1978). Digestibility can also be predicted from a quantitative knowledge of the various fibre fractions of the plant (Van der Koelen and Van Es, 1973) but with less accuracy.

The errors of prediction of *in vitro* digestibility from a range of methods are presented in Table 3.1. The N-regression technique and the *in vitro* procedures of Tilley and Terry (1963) provide the best predictions.

Subsequent workers have introduced modifications to the basic *in vitro* procedures (Van Soest *et al*, 1966; Engels and Van der Merwe, 1967).

Table 3.1   The accuracy of prediction of **in vivo** *digestibility*

Method	Forage	RSD	Reference
Pepsin-cellulase	Dried grasses	1.80	Terry *et al*, 1978
Rumen liquor-pepsin	Dried grasses	1.46	Terry *et al*, 1978
Pepsin-cellulase	Dried legumes	3.17	Terry *et al*, 1978
Rumen liquor-pepsin	Dried legumes	1.91	Terry *et al*, 1978
Pepsin-cellulase	Dried grasses & legumes	3.80	Terry *et al*, 1978
Rumen liquor-pepsin	Dried grasses & legumes	1.60	Terry *et al*, 1978
N-regression	Fresh grass	1.58	Vadiveloo & Holmes, 1979
N-regression	Fresh mixed grass/ legume herbage	0.90	Greenhalgh *et al*, 1960
N-regression	Fresh mixed grass/ legume herbage	1.50	Greenhalgh & Corbett, 1960.
Chromogen	Fresh mixed grass/ legume herbage	1.50	
Acid insoluble ash	Dried grass, legumes & grain	2.01–2.74	Van Keulen & Young, 1977
Cell wall constituents	Fresh grass	2.54	Van der Koelen & Van Es, 1973
Lignin	Fresh grass	Steers 2.4 Wethers 3.1	Forbes & Garrigus, 1950.

The major difficulty associated with each of these procedures is the initial selection of the material and the degree to which it represents that actually consumed by the grazing animal. The analytical procedures associated with these techniques are relatively sophisticated and, in the case of the Tilley and Terry method, require the maintenance of rumen fistulated donor animals to supply rumen liquor. Numerous arguments (Drew, 1966; Van Dyne and Weir, 1966; Scales *et al*, 1974) have been put forward pertaining to the optimal diet and the times at which rumen liquor is obtained from these donors. Much of the discussion has been based on the need to feed a diet similar to that being analysed in the laboratory; however the results on this point appear contradictory. With a large number of samples of different materials to be analysed, this is impractical and in general the animals, usually mature adults, are fed on medium/good quality hay, ensuring that nitrogen supply is adequate in order to provide a highly viable, mixed rumen microflora. In most cases the donor animals are sheep; it appears that rumen liquor obtained from these animals is satisfactory for use on diets being fed to other ruminants. The laboratory procedures are well documented elsewhere (Tilley and Terry, 1963) and will not be repeated here except to stress the necessity for running a range of standards of known *in vivo* digestibility with each batch of experimental samples to permit correction for batch variation. These standards should be of material comparable to that being examined. The material should be dried in the same manner as the samples and should be derived from diets fed at the same level of intake. If the variation in the estimated digestibility of the standards is too far from their *in vivo* value (at the Grassland Research Institute a value of 4% units), it is essential that the data be disregarded and the samples re-analysed.

Similarly, the procedures for the cellulase technique are documented (Jones and Hayward, 1975) and these will not be discussed further. Generally, when predicting digestibility from the Tilley and Terry *in vitro* method, the relationship is assumed to be unity (Terry *et al*, 1973). The assumption may not always be valid and various reported relationships are given in Table 3.2. However, it appears that the relationship between *in vitro* and *in vivo* digestibility reported by Tilley and Terry is more general than that for the cellulase technique where separate regressions are necessary for different species of forage. A specific regression may therefore have to be derived by an experimenter for his own particular circumstances when using the cellulase technique.

Table 3.2   *Regressions of* **in vivo** *(y) upon* **in vitro** *(x) OM digestibility (y = a + bx)*

Material	a	b	
Fresh grass and legumes	2.554	1.0182 RSD ± 1.904	Terry *et al*, (1973)
Fresh grass	11.92	0.850 r = 0.927	Van der Koelen and Dijkstra (1971)
Other fresh roughages	6.28	0.908 r = 0.981	
All roughages	5.77	0.920 r = 0.901	
Fresh grass	16.75	0.80 r = 0.72	Kellner & Kirchgessner (1976)
Fresh roughages and hay	5.05	0.97 r = 0.96	Alexander & McGowan (1966)
Fresh grass (Maintenance)	0	1.061 RSD ± 2.02	Valderrabano (1979)
(Above maintenance)	18.52	0.804 RSD ± 2.85	
(Extrusa — maintenance)	0	1.007 RSD ± 3.14	
(Extrusa — above maintenance)	−9.39	1.130 RSD ± 3.21	

3.4.4   The collection of samples of grazed herbage

Collection of samples representative of the herbage grazed is the essence of the success of the *in vitro* techniques and theoretically allows them to be of use in a far wider range of grazing circumstances than is the case with, for example, N-regression. If truly representative samples of herbage can be collected and analysed effectively, *in vitro* techniques should monopolise the whole area of intake estimation, from the strip-grazed homogeneous pasture to the multi-species range situation. However, the collection of these samples is not always simple.

There are two basic procedures for sample collection:

i) manual — by the experimenter, following close observation of the grazing animal.

ii) animal — by surgically prepared animals, fistulated in the oesophagus or the rumen.

Both procedures require that the samples are collected at a number of points through the grazing period to ensure the material is representative of that grazed.

The number and distribution of samplings necessary will depend on the potential range of digestibility in the material consumed. If the forage on offer is homogeneous and changes little through the period (for example on a set-stocked ryegrass pasture) and there is little diurnal selection by the animal, then sampling can be undertaken at any time and the number of samples collected need only be a reflection of the magnitude of the random variation and the degree of precision required. Conversely, on a range pasture from which the diet may be of grasses, legumes, herbs, shrubs and trees, the requirement for sampling will be far more complex, particularly when these different materials are consumed at different times of day, or even on different days during the grazing period. Any deviation from the simplest situation given in the first example above necessitates a decision as to what weighting to give the digestibility of any given sample relative to the total feed intake. For example, if cattle strip graze a pasture at a low herbage allowance and samples are taken for digestibility estimates close to the beginning and end of a day's allocation, then in the simplest situation the material sampled will be from horizons A and B respectively in Figure 3.1.

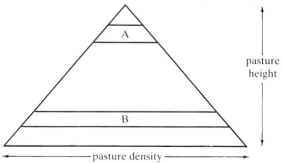

Fig. 3.1   Diagrammatic representation of grazed horizons of a pasture

There are two questions that must be answered: "Is the change in digestibility from A to B rectilinear or curvilinear?" and "What are the relative contributions from A and B to the whole diet?" The accepted procedure is to take a simple mean of A and B as the digestibility of the grass eaten. This assumes a rectilinear change in digestibility and no difference in the quantities selected from each horizon. If either of these assumptions is invalid for example if B is grass and A is the highly lignified leaves of a tropical shrub, then production of a composite value for an intake estimation may well prove difficult. In the context of multi-species pastures it may be more meaningful to characterise the quality of the various different plants and parts of plants that the grazing or browsing animals selects and then, from detailed behavioural observations of the time and intensity with which each species is consumed, derive the intake of individual forage plants (see Chapter 2).

These two examples of selection from different grazing conditions represent extremes, and most grazing trials will fall somewhere in between; but they do serve to demonstrate the thought which must be put into the various methods of sampling and how the chance of success will determine the ultimate decision on the overall method of intake measurement adopted.

3.4.4.1 *Manual collection.* The manual collection of herbage samples representative of that grazed by the animal requires the collector to observe precisely what plants and parts of plants the grazers are eating and then to mimic this selection by either plucking or cutting equivalent parts from similar plants with hand shears. A major decision must be taken as to when samples should be collected in order to provide a representative sample of the forage(s) being selected. This will obviously be determined to a large extent by the pattern of grazing imposed and/or type of pasture being studied. In situations where there is relatively little scope for selection (for example on a pasture continuously stocked at a high stocking rate) timing is not too critical, although manual collection from these pastures can be very slow and tedious. At the other extreme, on range pasture where animals may select different varieties and species at different times of the day, then sampling must span the spectrum of selection. This may require sampling to be carried out at intervals throughout days as well as over a number of days. It is in this context that the technique displays both its major strength and weakness. Strength, because the human sampler can collect any material at any time and as frequently as required provided time permits, whilst it is difficult to use surgically prepared animals at this level of sampling intensity without a very large resource input of fistulated animals. Weakness, because the more varied the selection possibilities, the more difficult it is to mimic the animal's behaviour.

The judgement of the operator is of paramount importance and dedication to the task essential. The technique is by definition subjective, but has been shown to work satisfactorily (Gibb and Treacher, 1976). However the animal often appears to select material higher in *in vitro* digestibility and N percentage than the experimenter. Such comparisons are normally made with material collected from fistulated animals and part of this observed discrepancy may be due to the addition of saliva to the fistula samples. However, bias of one technique relative to the other cannot be entirely ruled out.

Once collected, the samples of herbage should be frozen quickly to prevent deterioration, and stored to await drying, processing and analysis.

3.4.4.2 *Collection of fistula samples*. Techniques for the collection of samples of grazed herbage by animals fistulated in either the rumen (Tayler and Deriaz, 1963) or oesophagus (Torell, 1954; Hamilton *et al*, 1960) have been developed. With improvement in surgical techniques and the design of sample plugs, the oesophageal fistulate (OF) has superseded the use of rumen fistulates (RF). The whole process of collection with OF's is far simpler, necessitating only the removal of the plug and the hanging of a collection bag around the animal's neck during grazing. Sampling with the RF requires firstly the removal of part or all of the rumen contents in order to expose the point of entry of food into the rumen at the cardia and then its replacement after sampling. The animal is then allowed to graze whilst the experimenter inserts an arm through the fistula to catch the ingested material as it drops from the cardia. For this the animal must be very tame and the fistula large, which makes the technique impractical for sheep or young cattle. It is often difficult to prevent contamination of the freshly grazed material with rumen contents and the selection of tame animals may mean that they are not representative of the normal population.

Subsequent discussions will be centred upon the use of the OF for collection of grazed forage samples.

Legal requirements and ethical considerations govern the use of surgically-prepared animals in many countries and these aspects must be considered. In the United Kingdom all experiments with such animals come within the jurisdiction of the Cruelty to Animals Act, 1876.

The major scientific argument forwarded for the use of fistulated animals is that they overcome the major deficiency inherent in manual collection of "grazed" forage samples, that of subjective selection by the experimenter. This is incontrovertible BUT it is essential to be certain that the samples collected from these animals, after the inevitable mastication and saliva addition, can be obtained in a condition that does not impose some other bias on the subsequent analysis. These points are thoroughly discussed by Langlands (1975) who has shown that corrections for the addition of saliva may be necessary.

Description of the techniques for surgical preparation of fistulae are beyond the scope of this handbook but may be found in papers by Torell (1954) and Hamilton *et al* (1960). As important as the surgery is the after-care of the animals and their subsequent management, both on a routine day-to-day basis and during collection (see 3.9.2).

3.4.4.3 *Experimental design.* When using OF animals the selectivity of individuals may result in the variation between animals being larger than that between sampling times and treatments. For example, Langlands (1967a) reported a standard deviation of $\pm$ 1.6 digestibility units between sheep and $\pm$ 1.3 units between days with a value of $\pm$ 2.7 units for the combined sheep x day interaction and error term. The predominance of between animal variation strongly supports the use of experimental designs using OF's across grazing treatments that allow animal variation to be isolated and removed.

It seems likely that with simple swards or pasture conditions that do not impose extremes of grazing management, cross-over designs, with one or two animals per cell and short periods, can be employed. If mixed swards or more sharply contrasting pastures are to be examined then fistulated animals will need to be grazed on their test area throughout or perhaps even before the trial to offer adequate acclimatization. A minimum pre-sampling period of three weeks was suggested by Curll (1981). This will require an increase in animal numbers if the precision of estimation is to be maintained. On the basis of animal variation this was calculated to be as high as 12-fold by Hodgson (1969). However acclimatization may reduce between animal variation and hence the need for such large numbers. Decisions on design will depend upon the level of precision required, sward type and resources available.

3.4.4.4 *Working with fisulated animals.* The objective is to obtain a sample representative of the herbage being grazed by the main body of animals with the minimum of contamination by saliva. Every effort should be made to ensure that the OF animals graze in a manner typical of the main group. Therefore, they should be familiar with the plant association and general environment in order to avoid abnormal behaviour and biased selection; this is of particular importance on mixed swards. To ensure familiarisation it is advisable that OF animals are kept with the other live stock on the experimental pastures for as long as possible prior to sampling. Where this is not possible, some previous experience on similar areas is essential. The chances of obtaining a good sample are better if the times of collection coincide with those of maximum grazing activity in the herd or flock. This minimises interference with the fistulated animals by others in the field and ensures that all are keen to graze.

The collection procedure requires that the animal is restrained and its plug removed. Any extraneous material must then be cleared from around the fistula and a plastic bag attached around the neck. The animal is then allowed to graze. Care must be taken to ensure that the animal is not ruminating when the plug is removed or regurgitated material will enter the sampling bag. If rumination takes place during sampling or if water or any other materials (other than the sample forage) is consumed, the sample should be discarded. After sampling the animal is again restrained, the bag removed and the fistula plug re-inserted. The duration of the sampling period will be dependent upon the size of the sample required and the rate of eating. In general, the plug should not remain out of the fistula for more than $\frac{1}{2}$ hour or the orifice will shrink to a degree that may make plug re-insertion difficult.

Recoveries of ingested material in the extrusa are variable, depending on the physical characteristics of the forage being eaten and the size and attitude of the fistula; this can lead to unrepresentative sampling. The problem can be alleviated by inserting a foam rubber sponge in the lower oesophagus when sampling. However, animals must be trained to accept this plug as initially some may refuse to graze with it in place.

When ample forage is available, samples can be collected in a few minutes. However, when feed is scarce, obtaining a sample may prove difficult, particularly if the animals are loathe to graze. In such circumstances a further attempt must be made to collect a sample at another time or date. One practice frequently adopted is to pen the animals without food for a period of time prior to sampling to stimulate appetite. It can be argued that this "starvation" will modify the selection pressure exerted by the animal but there is no evidence to show other than very minor effects on the digestibility of the forage selected (Sidahmed *et al*, 1977).

Inherent in the collection of samples of grazed herbage by oesophageal fistulated animals is the contamination of these samples with saliva. The quantity added varies widely and is partly a function of the ease with which the animal can harvest herbage; the more difficult it is or the longer it takes to collect a suitable sized sample the more saliva will be added, since rate of salivary flow is relatively constant. The saliva cannot be removed from the sample without taking some of the soluble plant components with it and therefore reducing the digestibility of the whole sample. If the saliva is left in, a certain degree of contamination both with salivary salts and organic matter is inevitable. Even if digestibility is expressed on an organic matter basis, an over estimate will occur because the salivary organic matter is completely digestible. The degree of under or over estimation can be in the order of 3-4 and 1-2 units respectively (Langlands, 1966), and Gonzales and Lambourne (1966) reported increases in *in vitro* OM digestibility of up to 4.2 percentage units due to the addition of saliva.

Langlands (1967a) separated solid and liquid fractions of extrusa by squeezing through muslin and attempted to predict digestibility from values obtained for the two fractions. He concluded that samples containing a disproportionate amount of saliva should be discarded. It is therefore essential to adopt collection procedures that minimise salivary contamination of the samples. To make an estimate of the quantity of saliva added by the fistulated animals, samples of herbage should be taken at the same time that the fistulated animals are used to sample the pasture. The amount of water in the herbage sample and the extrusa sample is then measured and the difference between the quantities of water measured will give an estimate of the saliva added.

As soon as the sample has been collected it should be sealed in an air-tight bag and instantly frozen in dry ice (solid CO_2). Delays in freezing can result in continued digestion of soluble plant material by salivary enzymes and therefore in a net loss of dry matter, potentially leading to a depression in estimated digestibility. This is of particular relevance to very high digestibility crops.

3.4.4.5 *Processing the extrusa samples.* All samples for chemical analysis should be freeze-dried rather than oven-dried, to minimise the loss of volatile components, especially water soluble carbohydrates and nitrogen. This is of particular importance with extrusa samples in which a proportion of the cell contents has been released into the salivary fraction during mastication. The entire extrusa sample should be dried and then ground through a fine sieve (eg 0.8 mm) and any sub-sampling done on this material. To effectively sub-sample the frozen extrusa is difficult since the solid and liquid phases tend to freeze as separate fractions, not as one homogeneous mass. Since freeze drying leaves a sample of approximately 90% DM, correction of all subsequent analytical results to 100% DM has to be undertaken. This correction factor is best derived by oven drying a separate sample of the freeze-dried material at 100°C for 4 hours or by deriving a chemical dry matter using the Karl Fischer (Fischer 1935) technique.

Fine grinding of the samples is necessary to permit good mixing and to allow representative sub-samples to be taken for analysis, particularly as most analyses are carried out on samples of 0.5 g or less. The fineness of grinding is also important for the proper functioning of the *in vitro* technique. Particles of coarsely ground forage can float on the top of the digestion tubes, and even if these are shaken, the coarser particles may not be completely digested, thus biasing the estimation of digestibility downwards.

3.4.5 Interpretation and use of *in vitro* digestibility data

Whilst the various techniques described can be used to estimate *in vivo* digestibility of forage, the estimates are almost exclusively based upon *in vivo* determinations undertaken with wether sheep offered dried herbage only at the maintenance level of feeding. This base line is entirely satisfactory in, for example, agronomic comparisons between grass species or for ranking conserved forages. However, when a derived digestibility is used together with an estimation of faecal output for calculating herbage intake, other factors likely to influence the *in vivo* value should be taken into account. Chief amongst these are the effects of level of intake and the consumption of other feeds upon forage digestibility.

3.4.5.1 *Level of intake.* It is well recognised that as intake of a feed increases so its digestibility is reduced. The degree of reduction varies between feeds and has been shown to vary from 0-5 percentage units of digestibility per multiple of maintenance for fresh grass; this has obvious implications for the calculation of the amount of herbage eaten.

The size of the reduction in digestibility is not related to any quantifiable characteristic of the herbage and therefore no correction can be made at present. Neither can a correction be made until intake has been measured and the level of feeding established. Some feeding systems do recognise that the metabolisable energy (ME) of a forage for sheep is greater than for cattle and therefore, by implication, uncorrected results should be more in line for cattle.

For animals offered herbage *ad libitum* the effect of level of intake upon *in vivo* digestibility can be quite large with, it can be assumed, commensurately large effects on the estimation of intake. The publication Commonwealth Agricultural Bureau (1961) proposed a reduction of 1.5 percentage units of digestibility estimated *in vitro* when this value is used to calculate intake by grazing animals.

Langlands and Bennett (1973) used the equation given by Blaxter (1961) to correct the estimated intake of herbage by sheep. They assumed that the herbage had a digestibility equal to that at maintenance to make the initial calculation. The intake thus calculated was then corrected using the equation of Blaxter. This retrospective correction may also give rise to errors in estimating intake. Wilkins (1969) suggested a method for correcting for level of intake by using potentially digestible cellulose. He postulated that if cellulose digestibility *in vivo* (CD) were:

$$CD = \frac{100\,(PCD - FD)}{100 - FD} \tag{3.6}$$

where FD = the potential digestibility of cellulose in faeces (%)

PCD = potential digestibility of the cellulose in the diet (%)

Then organic matter intake (OMI) by grazing animals would be estimated by:

$$OMI = FCP \; \frac{100}{100 - CD} \cdot \frac{100}{CC} \tag{3.7}$$

where FCP = total faecal cellulose

CC = the cellulose content of the feed eaten (%)

The author suggests that this technique would allow intake to be calculated without relying on the relationship between *in vitro* and *in vivo* digestibility and would take into account differences between animals.

It has also been suggested that the relationship between *in vivo* and *in vitro* digestibility should be derived from animals fed *ad libitum* since in many grazing studies animals are offered an unlimited supply of herbage. However, intake and performance in indoor trials are generally below those observed at pasture so this would not entirely eliminate the problem but might provide a closer approximation in many cases.

3.4.5.2 *Associative effects of dietary ingredients.* When two or more feeds are offered, the digestion of one is not independent of the other. The degree to which one feed affects the other depends on their relative compositions. For example, when a cereal is offered with the forage, the availability of rapidly fermentable carbohydrate in the cereal will modify the rumen fermentation pattern to a degree dependent on the proportion of cereal in the total diet. Although the few observations that have been made with fresh grass indicate that the associative effects of other feeds are small, it is unreasonable to ignore them and to apply the digestibility coefficients derived from forage offered alone to that feed when offered as part of a more complex diet. The calculation of intake is based on indigestibility and this is more severely affected by any error than is digestibility. One procedure that has been used to examine this problem in indoor trials is to feed various ratios of the components of the complex diet and to determine the digestibility of each component (x_j) by simultaneous solution of the determinants of a series of equations:

$$a_{11}\,x_1 + a_{12}\,x_2 + \text{------} + a_{1n}\,x_n = k_1$$
$$a_{21}\,x_1 + a_{22}x_2 + \text{------} + a_{2n}\,x_n = k_2 \tag{3.8}$$
$$a_{n1}\,x_1 + a_{n2}\,x_2 + \text{------} + a_{nn}\,x_n = k_n$$

when a_{ij} = fraction of each ingredient in the ration
  x_j = digestibility of the ingredient in the ration
  k_j = digestibility of the total ration j

This approach was considered comprehensively by Kromann (1973). The method cannot be applied at pasture since the quantity of grass consumed is not known. It may be used, however, to assess the likely magnitude of any effects by cutting grass and feeding it indoors.

A solution for a two-component diet at pasture, the intake of one component of which is known, may be found in the use of an internal, indigestible dietary marker, used in combination with an external marker. If we use a grass/cereal diet as an example:

$$Ca_1 + Ga_2 = ta_3 \qquad\qquad (3.9)$$

where C = weight of cereal fed
  G = weight of grass consumed
  t = total weight of faeces, derived from Cr_2O_3 dilution procedure
  a_1, a_2, a_3 = concentration of marker in cereal, grass and total faeces
          respectively.

By manipulation

$$G = \frac{ta_3 - Ca_1}{a_2} \qquad\qquad (3.10)$$

This procedure does, of course, depend upon reliable determination of the internal marker as discussed earlier. A method of extrapolating the results of an indoor experiment to a grazing experiment to account for associative effects has been described by Milne et al (1981).

3.4.6 Nylon bag techniques

An alternative to the Tilley and Terry technique is the nylon bag technique. Samples of feed are placed in bags made of materials that are not digested by the enzymes produced in the rumen. The bags are introduced into the rumen via a fistula, left for a period of time, then removed and the disappearance of DM and/or OM is measured. The bags should be constructed of material having a pore size such that digestion can take place within the bag without loss of undigested particles of feed or ingress of extraneous indigestible material.

This technique was originally discussed by Quin et al (1938). Recent developments in the materials available, the manufacture of the bags, methods of closure, bag size, pore size and the relationship between sample size and bag size have led to improved predictions of *in vivo* digestibility using this technique. Aerts *et al* (1977) considered the nylon bag technique to be the best method of predicting *in vivo* organic matter digestibility of all the methods they investigated including the Tilley and Terry *in vitro* technique.

It is not possible to discuss the full details of the technique here and only an outline will be given but further details are contained in papers by Mehrez and Ørskov (1977), Aerts *et al* (1977), Van Hellen and Ellis (1977) and Demarquilly and Chenost (1969).

The bags are 200 mm long and 90 mm wide and made of polyester material; a suggested maximum pore size is 43 μm. The bags should be double seamed and the bottom rounded to prevent trapping of residues in the corners; the stitch holes should be sealed with silicon rubber.

The bag and bag plus sample are weighed (approximately 5 g of DM). The bag is then sealed and placed in the rumen for 48 hours. After this incubation period the bags are removed and washed with running tap water and then re-incubated for 48 hours at 39°C, in darkness, in a pepsin — H Cl solution, as described by Tilley and Terry (1963). They are again washed with running water before being dried and weighed and the ash content of the undigested residue determined. For each sample, digestibility is determined on two consecutive runs; standard samples are also included.

Using this technique on 42 grass hays of known *in vivo* digestibility, Aerts *et al* (1977) found the following relationships:

OMD (*in vivo*) = 13.5 + 0.69 OMD (measured by nylon bags) (3.11)
RSD ± 2.4

The regression found using the Tilley and Terry method was:
OMD (*in vivo*) = 12.4 + 0.82 OMD (*in vitro* Tilley and Terry) (3.12)
RSD ± 3.1

Advantages associated with this method are:
i)   Relatively large samples can be used (samples of up to 50 g of fresh herbage), thus avoiding changes in sample composition and digestibility that may be brought about by sample processing (Playne *et al*, 1978).
ii)   The nylon bag is in a large quantity of rumen fluid and therefore variability between samples of rumen fluid (as used in the Tilley and Terry technique) are less important.
iii)   The rumen liquor does not undergo any treatment prior to being used to digest the sample.

However, further work is required on this technique to try to establish more general relationships with *in vivo* digestibility.

3.4.7 Accuracy of digestibility estimates

3.4.7.1 *Ratio technique.* The ratio technique is subject to both bias and random error. Bias because recovery of the marker is generally assumed to be 100%, but rarely is, and random sampling error associated with both feed and faeces marker concentrations. There is also error in chemical determination of the marker. Streeter (1969) reviewed the errors associated with marker recovery. For example, a large variation was evident in the standard error of the recovery of lignin (CV 0.6 – 7.7%); this cannot however be used to calculate the error of prediction of digestibility. The extent of random variation in feed and faeces lignin concentration has not been reported and it is therefore not possible to quantify the total variation associated with this technique.

3.4.7.2 *Faecal index and **in vitro** techniques.* There are two sources of error with each of these techniques. The first is that involved with establishing the relationship between *in vivo* digestibility and in the one case faecal N concentration and in the other *in vitro* digestibility. A comparison of some of the RSDs reported for the relationships is given in Table 3.1. Their error becomes a bias when a relationship is used to predict digestibility.

The second source of error is that of either faecal or feed sampling, and analysis, and the subsequent prediction from the established relationship. Analytical error must be determined by the individual experimenter and will largely be governed by the tolerances acceptable in a particular laboratory. For example the authors have estimated their analytical error on OMD of herbage extrusa with a mean value of 75% to be $\pm$ 1.7% units (CV 2.3%).

Sampling error is predominately that occurring between animals. When using OF's to select samples of grazed herbage the between animal variation was estimated by the authors to be between 1 and 2% units, for cattle selecting material with a mean OMD of 78%.

The standard error of prediction of digestibility from any one of the equations in Table 3.1 can be derived from:

$$se = RSD \sqrt{\frac{1}{c} + \frac{1}{n_1} + \frac{(x_0 - \bar{x})^2}{n_1 \, Var\,(x)}} \qquad (3.13)$$

(after Raymond *et al* 1954),

where c is a number reflecting differences in the faecal collection methods
(ie numbers of animals used and length of collection period) used in
calculating the regression, and for prediction.
n_1 = number or observations upon which the regression is based

$\bar{x}$ and Var (x) are the mean and variance of the independent variable (nitrogen content or *in vitro* digestibility) used in calculating the regression

x_0 is the value of x used for prediction

The term $\dfrac{(x_0 - \bar{x})^2}{n_1 \text{ Var }(x)}$ allows for the shape of the confidence intervals of the regression line being wider at the extremes of the range. When n_1 is large both this term and $1/n_1$ tend to zero and therefore c becomes the principal determinant of the error of prediction.

If the same procedures are used, in animal numbers per treatment and periods of collection (for the grazing study as those used to derive the regression) then c = 1. Increasing either or both animal numbers and faecal collection period length will increase c, reduce $1/_c$ and improve the precision of the estimate of digestibility. Estimates of this improvement were given by Greenhalgh *et al* (1960) for the nitrogen regression procedure. For the *in vitro* technique c is solely dependent upon the number of animals used.

The total error of digestibility estimation from the N regression and *in vitro* procedures have been variously estimated. Examples are CVs of 2.4% at a digestibility of 70% (Raymond *et al*, 1954) for the former and 2.9–5.4% (Hodgson, 1969) with an average of 3.9% at a digestibility of 80% for the latter. These correspond with CVs of 5.7 and 15.6% for indigestibility.

From these data and those estimates of error associated with faecal output estimation, the total random error of intake estimation at a digestibility of 80% will be at least 11 and 15% when faecal-index and oesophageal fistulate procedures respectively are used.

3.5 WEIGHING ANIMALS

Weighing animals to estimate intake over short periods of time was suggested by Erizian (1932):

$$\text{Intake} = (Wt_2 + F + U + I) - Wt_1 - L \qquad (3.14)$$

where Wt_1 and Wt_2 are liveweights before and after a period of grazing,
F and U are the weights of faeces and urine voided during the period of grazing
I is the 'insensible loss of weight'
L is the weight of water drunk.

To use this method, animals are fitted with harnesses and dung bags for faeces collection and containers for urine collection. The animals are weighed and then turned out to graze and any water consumption is measured. After grazing, the animals are weighed again and faeces and urine production are also measured. Other animals, that are harnessed for the measurement of faeces and urine production but not allowed to graze, are also weighed before and after the grazing period to estimate 'insensible loss of weight'. However, as these animals are likely to be less active than those grazing, the 'insensible loss of weight' may be underestimated. This method was used in a slightly modified form by Allden and Young (1959).

Horn (1978; personal communication 1979) fitted load cells to the feet of cattle in order to continuously monitor the weight change of the animals. The data were transmitted using ratio telemetry and estimates of intake could be made.

In both the above methods of measuring intake an estimate of fresh herbage consumption is obtained. Samples of herbage selected by the animals have to be taken to obtain estimates of the dry matter and organic matter content of the diet selected. This method may be useful to estimate intake over short periods and could be used to calculate mean bite size when used in connection with rate of biting measurements (see Chapter 6).

3.6 WATER TURNOVER

Benjamin *et al* (1975) described a method to estimate food intake by grazing sheep under arid conditions when no free water is available.

The animals were fasted for 18 hours and given an injection of 200 μCi of tritiated water (TOH) made up in sterile saline. A venous blood sample was taken 6-7 hours after injection for total body water (TBW) determination (Till and Downes, 1962). Subsequent blood samples were taken on each of 5 grazing days at the same hour. The water turnover was estimated by following the decrease in radioactivity and was assumed to represent water intake from the herbage. A mean DM of herbage samples was used to calculate the daily DM intake by solving the following equation:

$$DMI = \frac{X}{Y} \times Z \qquad\qquad (3.15)$$

where DMI = kg of DM intake/24 hours
     X = litres of water turnover/24 hours
     Y = % water content of pasture
     Z = % DM of pasture

The authors concluded that under their conditions, fresh matter and dry matter intakes could be confidently estimated using this method and the mean intakes were similar to those obtained by cutting quadrats before and after grazing.

In a further experiment Benjamin *et al* (1977) modified this technique. They calculated a relationship between herbage intake and food water (tritiated water space minus water drunk) using caged sheep fed material similar to that offered to grazing animals. Herbage intake of the grazing animals was then calculated using this relationship and measured food-water intake of the grazing animals.

This modification of the technique would give rise to difficulties that are common to other methods requiring parallel feeding trials and thus the main advantages of this technique appear to have been lost.

3.7 CONCLUSIONS AND FUTURE DEVELOPMENTS

It can be concluded from the techniques described that animal-based methods of estimating intake are generally least reliable when short-term measurements (<3 days) are required, and are more suited to conditions where herbage intake and digestibility are relatively constant. However, within the limitations of the procedures described it has been possible to examine many of the gross factors affecting herbage intake. More precise techniques must be developed to allow closer definition of the complex relationships between the grazing animals and its feed source, the sward. As a first step if total faeces were collected and a suitable internal marker were found, then accuracy of predicting intake could be improved.

The possibility of using plant silica is being re-examined. In indoor experiments silica has been found to be a suitable marker for cattle and sheep (Van Keulen and Young, 1977) but at pasture larger intakes of silica from the soil may vitiate the use of this technique. However, plants contain little titanium (<1 ppm, Healy, 1968) and titanium is not absorbed by the animal. If the ratio of silica to titanium in the soil is measured and this ratio is relatively constant over the area which the animals are grazing then soil silica in both feed selected and faeces produced by the animal could be estimated from the titanium present. Such a technique does not however remove the need to collect a sample of pasture as grazed by the animal.

Preliminary results reported by Grace and Body (1981) have shown that long chain (C_{19}–C_{32}) fatty acids in herbage may also be suitable internal markers but this technique has yet to be tried over a range of samples.

Another possible internal marker is potentially indigestible cellulose (PIC). The method suggested by Wilkins (1969) described earlier seems unnecessarily complicated. If potentially indigestible cellulose measured in the feed is totally recoverable in the faeces derived from that feed, then this would be a suitable marker. Intake could then be calculated as:

$$\text{Feed intake} = \frac{\text{Faecal output x concentration of PIC in faeces}}{\text{Concentration of PIC in feed}} \quad (3.16)$$

Recent work (Penning, unpublished data) has shown that when feeds and faeces are placed in polyester bags and introduced into the rumen of animals, the weight of cellulose in the sample reaches a constant value after about ten days for samples of feed and faeces. This technique has yet to be tried over a wide range of samples and different levels of intake.

The estimation of faeces output may also be improved by the development of equipment to supply continuous doses of a marker and Laby (personal communication) in Australia is working on the development of such systems.

3.8 REFERENCES

AERTS, J V, DE BRABANDER, D L, COTTYN, B G and BUYSSE, F X (1977). Comparison of the laboratory methods for predicting the organic matter digestibility of forages. *Animal Feed, Science and Technology*, 2, 337-349.

ALEXANDER, R H and McGOWAN, M (1966). The routine determination of the *in vitro* digestibility of organic matter in forages. An investigation of the problems associated with continuous large-scale operation. *Journal of the British Grassland Society*, 21, 140-147.

ALDEN, W G and YOUNG, R S (1959). The summer nutrition of weaner sheep: Herbage intake following periods of differential nutrition. *Australian Journal of Agricultural Research*, 15, 989-1000.

ANON (1977). Rowett Research Institute, *Annual Report on Studies in Animal Nutrition and Allied Sciences*, 33, pp 59.

BENJAMIN, R W, CHEN, M, DEGEN, A A, ABDUL AZIZ, N and AL HADAD, M J (1977). Estimation of the dry- and organic-matter intake of young sheep grazing a dry Mediterranean pasture, and their maintenance requirements. *Journal of Agricultural Science, Cambridge*, 88, 513-520.

BENJAMIN, R W, DEGEN, A A, BREIGHET, A, CHEN, M and TADMORE, N H (1975). Estimation of food intake of sheep grazing green pasture when no free water is available. *Journal of Agricultural Science, Cambridge*, 85, 403-407.

BLAXTER, J L (1961). The utilization of energy of food by ruminants. *Proc 2nd Symposium on Energy Metabolism EAAP Publication No 100*, pp 211-225.

BLAXTER, K L, WAINMAN, F W and DAVIDSON, J L (1966). The voluntary intake of food by sheep and cattle in relation to their energy requirements for maintenance. *Animal Productions*, 8, 75-83.

BRISSON, G J, PIGDEN, W J and SYLVESTER, S E (1957). Effect of frequency of administration of chromic oxide on its faecal excretion pattern by grazing cattle. *Canadian Journal of Agricultural Science*, 37, 90-94

BROWN, E and DUVAL, J W T (1907). A quick method for the determination of moisture in grain. *USDA Bureau Plant Industry, Bulletin No 99*.

CAMMELL, S B (1977). Equipment and techniques used for research into the intake and digestion of forages by sheep and calves. *Grassland Research Institute Technical Report, No. 24*.

COMMONWEALTH AGRICULTURAL BUREAUX (1961). Research techniques in use at the Grassland Research Institute, Hurley. *Bulletin 45, Publication Commonwealth Bureaux of Pasture Field Crops, Farnham Royal, Bucks, UK*.

COOP, I E and HILL, M K (1962). The energy requirements of sheep for maintenance and gain. II Grazing sheep. *Journal of Agricultural Science Cambridge*, 58, 187-199.

CORBETT, J L, GREENHALGH, J F D and McDONALD, A P (1958). Paper as a carrier of chromium sesquioxide. *Nature, London*, 182, 1014-1016.

CORBETT, J L, GREENHALGH, J F D and FLORENCE, E (1959). Distribution of chromium sesquioxide and polyethyleneglycol in the reticulo-rumen of cattle. *British Journal of Nutrition*, 13, 337-345

CURLL, M L (1981). The effect of grazing by set-stocked sheep on a perennial ryegrass/white clover pasture. *Ph D Thesis, University of Reading*.

DEMARQUILLY, G and CHENOST, M (1969). Etude de la digestion des fourrages dans le rumen par la méthode des sachets de nylon. Liaisons avec le valeur alimentaire. *Annals Zootechnie*, 18, 419-436.

DREW, K R (1966). The *in vitro* prediction of herbage digestibility. *Proceedings New Zealand Society of Animal Production*, 26, 52-70.

EDIN, H (1918), cited by Kotb and Luckey (1972). *Nutritional Abstracts & Reviews*, 42, 813-845.

ENGELS, E A N and VAN DER MERWE, F J (1967). Application of an *in vitro* technique to South African forages with special reference to the effect of certain factors on the results. *South African Journal of Agricultural Sciences*, 10, 983-995.

ERIZIAN, E (1932), Eine neue Methode zur Bestimmung der vom Vieh gefressenen Menge Weidefutters *Z Zucht*, 25, 443-459.

FISCHER, K (1935). Neues Verfahren zur massanalytischen Bestimmung des Wassergehaltes von Flüssigkeiten und festen Körpern. *Agnew Chem*, 487, 394-396.

FORBES, R M and GARRIGUS, W P (1950). Nutritive value and intake of grazed forages. *Journal of Animal Science*, 9, 354-362.

GIBB, M J and TREACHER, T T (1976). The effect of herbage allowance on herbage intake and performance of lambs grazing perennial ryegrass and red clover swards. *Journal of Agricultural Science, Cambridge*, 86, 355-365.

GONZALES, V and LAMBOURNE, J L (1966). Caracteristicas de la secrecion salivar de corderos alimentados con diferentes forrajes y efectos de la saliva sobre la digestibilidad "in vitro" de los mismos. *Revista de Nutricion Animal*, IV, 34-40.

GRACE, N D and BODY, D R (1981). The possible use of long chain fatty acids in herbage as an indigestible faecal marker. *Journal of Agricultural Science, Cambridge*, 97, 743-745.

GREENHALGH, J F D and CORBETT, J L (1960). The indirect estimation of the digestibility of pasture herbage. I. Nitrogen and chromagen as faecal index substances. *Journal of Agricultural Science, Cambridge*, 55, 371-376.

GREENHALGH, J F D, CORBETT, J L and McDONALD, I (1960). The indirect estimation of the digestibility of pasture herbage. II. Regressions of digestibility on faecal nitrogen concentration; their determination in continuous digestibility trials and the effect of various factors on their accuracy. *Journal of Agricultural Science, Cambridge*, 55, 377-386.

HAMILTON, F J, McMANUS, W R and LARSEN, L H (1960). An improved method of oesophageal fistulation for food intake studies in sheep. *Australian Veterinary Journal*, 36, 111-112.

HARDISON, W A and REID, J T (1953). Use of indicators in the measurement of dry-matter intake of grazing animals. *Journal of Nutrition*, 51, 35-52.

HARRIS, L E, LOFGREEN, G P, KERCHER, C J, RALEIGH, R J and BOHMAN, V R (1967). Techniques of research in ranch livestock nutrition. *Utah Agricultural Experimental Station Bulletin*, No 471.

HEALY, W B (1968). Ingestion of soil by dairy cows. *New Zealand Journal of Agricultural Research*, 11, 487-499.

HODGSON, J (1969). The use of sheep fitted with oesophageal fistulae in grazing studies. *Journal of the British Grassland Society*, 24, 325-332.

HORN, F (1978). Boots for cows. *Agricultural Research USDA*, September 1978, pp 12-13.

JONES, D I H and HAYWARD, M V (1975). The effect of pepsin pretreatment of herbage on the prediction of dry matter digestibility from solubility in fungal cellulase solution. *Journal of Science, Food and Agriculture*, 26, 711-718.

KELLNER, R J and KIRCHGESSNER, M (1976). Zur *in vitro* Bestimmung der Verdaulichkeit von Grunund Rauhfutter. *Das Wirtschaftseigner Futter*, 22, 157-166.

KOTB, A R and LUCKEY, T D (1972). Markers in Nutrition. *Nutrition Abstracts and Reviews*, 42, 813-845.

KROMANN, R P (1973). The energy value of feeds as influenced by associative effects. *Proceedings 1st International Green Crop Drying Conference*.

LAMBOURNE, L J (1957). Measurement of feed intake of grazing sheep. II. The estimation of faeces output using markers. *Journal of Agricultural Science, Cambridge*, 48, 415-425.

LANGLANDS, J P (1966). Studies on the nutritive value of the diet selected by grazing sheep. I. Difference in composition between herbages consumed and material collected from oesophageal fistula. *Animal Production*, 8, 253-259.

LANGLANDS, J P (1967a). Studies on the nutritive value of the diet selected by grazing sheep. II. Some sources of error when sampling oesophageally fistulated sheep at pasture. *Animal Production*, 9, 167-175.

LANGLANDS, J P (1967b). Studies on the nutritive value of the diet selected by grazing sheep. III. A comparison of oesophageal fistula and faecal index techniques for the indirect estimation of digestibility. *Animal Production*, 9, 325-331.

LANGLANDS, J P (1975). Techniques for estimating nutrient intake and its utilization by the grazing ruminant. In: *Digestion and metabolism in the ruminant*. Ed I W MacDonald, A C I Warner, Proceedings 4th International Symposium of Ruminant Nutrition 1974, pp 420-432. Univ New England, Australia.

LANGLANDS, J P and BENNETT, L L (1973). Stocking intensity and pastoral production. II. Herbage intake of Merino sheep grazed at different stocking rates. *Journal of Agricultural Science, Cambridge*, 81, 205-209.

LANGLANDS, J P, CORBETT, J L, McDONALD, I and REID, G W (1963a). Estimation of the faeces output of grazing animals from the concentration of chromium sesquioxide in a sample of faeces. I. Comparison of estimates from samples taken at fixed times of day with faeces output measured directly. *British Journal of Nutrition*, 17, 211-218.

LANGLANDS, J P, CORBETT, J L, McDONALD, I and REID, G W (1963b). Estimation of the faeces output of grazing animals from the concentration of chromium sesquioxide in a sample of faeces.

II. Comparison of estimates from samples taken at fixed times of the day with estimates of samples collected from the sward. *British Journal of Nutrition, 17*, 219-226.

LESPERANCE, A L and BOHMAN, V R (1961). Apparatus for collecting excreta from grazing cattle. *Journal of Animal Science, 20*, 503-505.

McDOUGALL, E I (1948). Studies on ruminant saliva. I. The composition and output of sheep's saliva. *Biochemistry Journal, 43, 99-109.*

MEHREZ, A A and ØRSKOV, E R (1977). A study of the artificial fibre bag technique for determining the digestibility of feeds in the rumen. *Journal of Agricultural Science, Cambridge, 88*, 645-650.

MICHELL, A R (1977). An inexpensive metabolic harness for female sheep. *British Veterinary Journal,* 133, 483-485.

MILNE, J A. MAXWELL, T J and SOUTER, W (1981). Effect of supplementary feeding and herbage mass on the intake and performance of grazing ewes in early lactation. *Animal Production, 32*, 185-195.

MINSON, D J and KEMP, C D (1961). Studies on the digestibility of herbage. *Journal of the British Grassland Society,* 16, 76-79.

MINSON, D J and RAYMOND, W F (1958). Sources of error in the use of faecal index relationships. *Experiments in Progress 10, 1956-1957,* Publication Grassland Research Institute, Hurley, pp 92-96.

MINSON, D J, TAYLER, J C, ALDER, F E, RAYMOND, W F, RUDMAN, J E, LINE, C and HEAD, M J (1960). A method for identifying the faeces produced by individual cattle on groups of cattle grazing together. *Journal of the British Grassland Society,* 15, 86-88.

MORAN, J B and GOMEZ, P O (1977). The production of chromic oxide paper pellets for use with young grazing cattle. *Journal of the British Grasskland Society,* 32, 49-50.

MORGAN, J P, PIENAAR, J P and CLARK, R A (1976). Animal based methods of determining herbage intake and quality under grazing conditions. *Proceedings of the Grasslands Society of South Africa,* 11, 73-78.

PENNING, P D and GIBB, M J (1979). The effect of milk intake on the intake of cut and grazed herbage by lambs. *Animal Production, 29,* 53-67.

PIGDEN, W J and BRISSON, G J (1956). Effect of frequency of administration of chromic oxide on its faecal excretion pattern by grazing wethers. *Canadian Journal of Agricultural Science, 36,* 146-155.

PLAYNE, M J (1978). Differences between cattle and sheep in their digestion and relative intake of a mature tropical grass hay. *Animal Feed Science & Technology,* 3, 41-49.

PLAYNE, M J, KHUMNUAYTHONG, W and ECHEVARRIA, M G (1978). Factors affecting the digestion of oesophageal fistula samples and hay samples in nylon bags in the rumen of cattle. *Journal of Agricultural Science, Cambridge,* 90, 193-204.

QUIN, J I, VAN DER WATH, J G and MYBURGH, S (1938). Studies on the alimentary tract of Merino sheep in South Africa. 4. Description of experimental technique. *Onderstepoort Journal of Veterinary Science and Animal Industry,* 11, 341-360.

RAYMOND, W F, KEMP, C D, KEMP, A W and HARRIS, C E (1954). Studies in the digestibility of herbage. IV. The use of faecal collection and chemical analysis in pasture studies. b) Faecal index methods. *Journal of the British Grassland Society,* 9, 69-82.

RAYMOND, W F and MINSON, D J (1955). The use of chromic oxide for estimating the faecal production of grazing animals. *Journal of the British Grassland Society,* 10, 282-296.

ROYAL, W M (1968). Equipment for collection of faeces from sheep. *Proceedings of the Australian Society of Animal Production,* 7, 450-454.

SCALES, G H, STREETER, C L, DENHAM, A H and WARD, G M (1974). A comparison of indirect methods of predicting *in vivo* digestibility of grazed forage. *Journal of Animal Science,* 38, 192-199.

SCHILD, G J and HONIG, H (1975). Methodische Untersuchungen zur Bewertung von Grundfutter. I. Teil: Schnellbestimmung des Trockenmassegehalts im Grundfutter Ber. *Ldw,* 393-401

SCHNEIDER, B H and FLATT, W P (1975). The evaluation of feeds through digestibility experiments. Publication *The University of Georgia Press,* Athens 30602 USA.

SIDAHMED, A E, MORRIS, J G, WEIR, W C and TORRELL, D T (1977). Effect of length of fasting on intake, *in vitro* digestibility and chemical composition of forage samples collected by oesophageal fistulated sheep. *Journal of Animal Science,* 45, 885-890.

STEVENSON, AUDREY E (1962). Measurement of intake by grazing cattle and sheep. VIII. Some observations on the accuracy of the chromic oxide technique for the estimation of faeces output of grazing cattle. *New Zealand Journal of Agricultural Research,* 5, 339-345.

STEVENSON, AUDREY E and CLARE, N T (1963). Measurement of feed intake by grazing cattle and sheep. IX. Determination of chromic oxide in faeces using an Auto-Analyser. *New Zealand Journal of Agricultural Research,* 6, 121-126.

STEVENSON, AUDREY E and de LANGEN, H (1960). Measurement of intake by grazing cattle and sheep. VII. Modified wet digestion method for determination of chromic oxide in faeces. *New Zealand Journal of Agricultural Research,* 3, 314-319.

STREETER, C L (1969). A review of techniques used to estimate the *in vivo* digestibility of grazed forage. *Journal of Animal Science,* 29, 757-768.

TAN, T N, WESTON, R H and HOGAN, J P (1971). Use of [103]Ru-labelled tris (1,10-phenanthroline). Ruthenium (II) Chloride as a marker in digestion studies with sheep. *International Journal of Applied Radiation and Isotopes*, 22, 301-308.

TAYLER, J C and DERIAZ, R E (1963). The use of rumen fistulated steers in the direct determination of nutritive value of ingested herbage in grazing experiments. *Journal of the British Grassland Society*, 18, 29-38.

TERRY, R A, MUNDELL, D C and OSBOURN, D F (1978). Comparison of two *in vitro* procedures using rumen liquor-pepsin or pepsin-cellulase for prediction of forage digestibility. *Journal of the British Grasslands Society*, 33, 13-18.

TERRY, R A, OSBOURN, D F, CAMMELL, S B and FENLOW, J S (1973). *In vitro* digestibility and the estimation of energy in herbage. *Vaxtodling*, 28, 19-25.

THEURER, C B (1970). Chemical indication techniques for determining range forage consumption. In: Range and Wildlife habitat. *USDA Miscellaneous Publications*, 1147, 220 pp.

TILL, A R, DOWNES, A M (1962). The measurement of total body water in sheep. *Australian Journal of Agricultural Research*, 13, 335-342.

TILLEY, M A and TERRY, R A (1963). A two-stage technique for the *in vitro* digestion of forage crops. *Journal of the British Grassland Society*, 18, 104-111.

TORELL, D T (1954). An oesophageal fistula for animal nutrition studies. *Journal of Animal Science*, 13, 878-884.

TROELSEN, J E (1963). Note on chromic oxide paper pellets for administration to ruminants. *Canadian Journal of Animal Science*, 43, 389-390.

TROELSEN, J E (1966). Pelleting of chromic oxide for administration to cattle and sheep. *Canadian Journal of Animal Science*, 46, 226-227.

VALDERRABANO, J (1979). Techniques of measuring intake by grazing sheep. *M Phil Thesis, University of Reading*.

VAN DER KOELEN, C J and DIJKSTRA, N D (1971). The *in vitro* digestion as a help in the evaluation of the nutritive value of roughages. *Landbouwk Tijdschr, S-Grav*, 83, 494-499.

VAN DER KOELEN, C J and VAN ES, A J H (1973). A comparison of some laboratory techniques for the estimation of the digestibility of the organic matter in forage samples. *Netherlands Journal of Agricultural Science*, 21, 199-205.

VAN DYNE, G M and WEIR, W C (1966). Comparisons of micro-digestion techniques under range and dry lot conditions. *Journal of Agricultural Science, Cambridge*, 67, 381-387.

VAN HELLEN, R W and ELLIS, W C (1977). Sample container porosities for rumen *in situ* studies. *Journal of Animal Science*, 44, 141-146.

VAN KEULEN, J and YOUNG, B A (1977). Evaluation of acid-insoluble ash as a natural marker in ruminant digestibility studies. *Journal of Animal Science*, 44, 282-287.

VAN SOEST, P J, WINE, R H and MOORE, L A (1966). Estimation of the true digestibility of forages by the *in vitro* digestion of cell walls. *Proceedings 10th International Grassland Congress*, pp. 438-441.

WATSON, M J and LABY, R H (1978). The response of grazing cattle to Monensin administered from a controlled release capsule. *Proceedings of the Nutrition Society, Australia*, 3, 86.

WILKINS, R J (1969). The potential digestibility of cellulose in forage and faeces. *Journal of Agricultural Science, Cambridge*, 73, 57-64.

WILLIAMS, C H, DAVID, D J and IISMAA, O (1962). The determination of chromic oxide in faeces samples by atomic absorption spectrophotometry. *Journal of Agricultural Science, Cambridge*, 59, 381-385.

VADIVELOO, J and HOLMES, W (1979). Supplementary feeding of grazing beef cattle. *Grass and Forage Science*, 34, 173-179.

3.9 APPENDICES

3.9.1 Chemical determination of chromic oxide

3.9.1.1 *Determination of Cr_2O_3 in faeces*

(1) Heat a disposable aluminium dish (Townson & Mercer 254-505) in furnace at 550°C to constant weight (2-3 hours).

(2) Cool, transfer to desiccator, number the lip of dish with lead pencil, and weigh to nearest milligram.

(3) Add 0.5-1.0 g sample (depending on approximate Cr_2O_3 content is known), and dry in oven at 100°C for 4 hours.

(4) Transfer to desiccator, cool and weigh to nearest milligram.
(5) Transfer to a cool muffle furnace and ash at 550°C overnight.
(6) Cool, transfer to desiccator and reweigh. Calculate weight and percentage ash.
(7) Transfer the ash with the MINIMUM quantity of water, to a 100 cm^3 conical flask. The dish can be folded inwards to ease the transfer. Light ashes may require damping with 2-3 drops of water before transfer to avoid scattering.
(8) Add a few anti-bumping granules and 6 cm^3 sulphuric/phosphoric acid mixture from an Oxford pipe or Transfer flask to a hot plate at 280-290°C.
(9) When boiling steadily add 3 cm^3 4.5% potassium bromate solution and continue heating.
(10) When boiling and effervescence have ceased the flask can be 'rolled' on its side to wash down any solids which may have crept up the sides of the flask.
(11) Continue heating until the colour of the solution is a deep purple, and white fumes are produced.
(12) Heat for a further 2-3 minutes then remove from heat and allow to cool.
(13) Add 97 cm^3 H$_2$O using dispenser set at 19.35 g speed 6.5 aliquots per flask. Cap with parafilm and shake.
(14) For short periods the solutions may be kept in the capped flasks. For longer periods store an aliquot in 30 cm^3 vials.

3.9.1.2 *Determination of Cr$_2$O$_3$ in capsules*

(1) Dry nickel crucibles at 100°C for 2 hours. Transfer to desiccator, cool and weigh.
(2) Place one (or more depending on size) capsule in crucible and reweigh.
(3) Heat on boiling ring until paper charred and no more fumes evolved. Take care not to allow the paper to ignite.
(4) Ash in muffle furnace at 550°C overnight.
(5) Cool, transfer to desiccator and reweigh. Calculate weight of ash.
(6) Grind ash with glass rod until fine and homogenous. Dry at 110°C for 1 hour.
(7) Weigh approximately 0.15 g (to the nearest 0.0001 g) into 100 cm^3 flask. Add 1 cm^3 1M sodium hydroxide solution and evaporate to dryness on water bath or 100°C hotplate (triplicate analysis of ash).
(8) Add antibumping granules, 18.0 cm^3 digestion acid mixture and bring to boil. Add 6 cm^3 4.5% potassium bromate solution. Carry out digestion as for faeces.
(9) Cool and transfer to 100 cm^3 volumetric flasks and make up to volume.

(10) Dilute 1 x 10 with 6% digestion acid.
(11) Ash some pure chromic oxide at the same time and treat as above. Calculate percentage recovery which should be 97-103%.

Reagents
Sulphuric/phosphoric acid mixture
1000 cm^3 H$_2$O
 500 cm^3 88% orthophosphoric acid SG 1.75 (H$_3$PO$_4$)
 100 cm^3 10% w/v manganese sulphate (MnSO$_4$)
Mix thoroughly.
Add 500 cm^3 concentrated sulphuric acid in small aliquots with constant swirling of the mixture.

Standards
    The standards are solutions of potassium dichromate equivalent to 2-150 μg cm^{-3} Cr$_2$O$_3$
Stock solution 0.5 mg cm^{-3}
0.9679 g oven dried (100°C for 4 hours). A.R. potassium dichromate dissolved in H$_2$O and made up to 1 cm^3.

Working standards μg cm^{-3}	Volume stock cm^3
2	1.0
5	2.5
10	5.0
25	12.5
50	25.0
100	50.0
150	75.0

    Dispense the above volumes into 250 cm^3 volumetric flasks from a burette. Add about 50 cm^3 H$_2$O, 15.0 cm^3 digestion acid and make up to volume with deionised water.

Atomic absorption spectrophotometric determination of chromium

    Measure chromium concentration on digests by direct aspiration (without dilution) into a nitrous oxide — acetylene flame.

Lamp current	25 mA
Absorption line	429.0 nm
Slit width	0.7 nm
Burner position	optimise for maximum absorption

Flame stoichiometry   optimise for maximum absorption
Integration time   3.5 sec

Standardise on H_2O (AZ), 25 μg cm^{-3} (S1), 150 μg cm^{-3} (S2). For low ranges use a more sensitive absorption line (425.4 nm or 357.9 nm), such that the top standard of the suitable range gives an absorbance of 0.500-0.700.

3.9.2   Care of fisulated animals

For the routine care of OF animals the following equipment should always be kept readily to hand:

1. Bucket, sponge and antiseptic solution.
2. Spare plugs and spacers.
3. Elastrator rings or other small, strong rubber bands.
4. Small scissors and sharp knife or scalpel. Long clamp forceps.
5. Surgical lubricant and antiseptic cream.
6. Artificial saliva (McDougall, 1948):

> Dissolve 18.5 g di-sodium hydrogen orthophosphate anhydrous and 49.0 g sodium hydrogen carbonate in a little distilled water. Then dissolve 47.9 g sodium chloride ($6H_2O$) and 4.0 g anhydrous calcium chloride to give 2 litres of aqueous solution. Add 100 ml of this chloride solution to the phosphate and bicarbonate and make up the volume to 1 litre with distilled water. (N.B. The chloride solution must be added after the phosphate and bicarbonate have been dissolved). This provides the "stock" solution; immediately before use dilute one part of stock solution with four parts of distilled water.

It is necessary to ensure that the area surrounding any fistula is kept clean; the frequency of cleaning will depend upon how much seepage takes place. It is also advisable to regularly clip away the wool/hair surrounding the fistula, and from the areas onto which leakage occurs, to facilitate cleaning.

Although all plugs are made of surgically inert material, abscesses can and do develop at the borders of the fistula (see 3.9.2.2). Regular inspection of the animals to ensure that no blockage or loss of plug has occurred is essential. If plugs are lost the "tone" in the muscle surrounding the fistula causes the hole to shrink, in some cases very rapidly; a long period without a plug can make it extremely difficult, if not impossible, to re-insert the plug. Inspection must, therefore, be on at least a daily basis and preferably twice per day; more frequent observation is necessary in the period immediately following initial surgery.

3.9.2.1 *Feeding.* In addition to adopting the principles of first-class husbandry when managing the animals, thought must be given to the types of diet made available. Water should be available at all times, together with salt-licks. These are essential for the maintenance of electrolyte balance, since salivary losses can be quite high. Long, fibrous forage may wrap around the OF plug, the resultant build up of material either blocking the oesophagus and all subsequent attempts to eat and ruminate or causing the fistula plug to be drawn in and swallowed. Care must therefore be taken, particularly in the early post-operative stages, in the selection of feeds and bedding materials. The swallowing of plugs may also occur when large, hard concentrate pellets are fed; very rapid consumption can "knock" the plug out of place and cause it to be swallowed. Freshly cut or grazed grass, chopped forage and "loose" cereal or concentrate mixes are therefore the most suitable feeds to offer OF animals if blockage problems are to be minimised, and in young animals an extended period of milk feeding facilitates post-operative recovery and minimises the occurrence of blockages.

3.9.2.2 *Fistula problems and problem solving.* Some of the major problems encountered when keeping OF animals, and the possible solutions to these, are documented below:

Blockage

Most blockages are caused by feed or ingested bedding. In the immediate post-operative phase, considerable swelling around the site of the fistula excaberates this problem. If the oesophagus is completely blocked the animal is often seen to cough and to salivate profusely. To clear such blockages, remove the plug and extract all the offending material from the oesophagus (if necessary with forceps) both above and below the fistula. Ensure that the animal can swallow satisfactorily and then replace the plug. If it is evident that a particular material is causing the problem, exclude it from the diet.

Swallowed plugs

This generally follows partial blockage and subsequent strong, peristaltic movement in the oesophagus.

(a) Complete — the plug may pass straight through into the rumen; here it will remain and can do no further harm. Simply replace the plug.

(b) Plug lodged in lower oesophagus — attempt to extract the plug with forceps or, if very far down and impossible to extract, attempt to push it through into the rumen. This latter operation should be undertaken with veterinary supervision. Should the plug be completely immovable, the animal must be slaughtered immediately.

Persistent swallowing of plugs can sometimes be combated by tying the plug around the animal's neck with a cord.

External loss of plug

Plugs may occasionally be pulled out on fences, etc or pushed out by large boluses of food or digesta. This is more likely to occur if the plug is not a good fit in the fistula, or the "wings" have become weakened with age. In the latter case, simply replacing it with a new plug will prevent recurrence but in the former, addition of spacers may be necessary. If the fistula becomes very large an additional form of closure can be used. A modified rumen cannula is inserted in the fistula and the 'L' shaped OF plugs are placed inside this; the securing rubber rings are then placed around the whole plug.

Restricted fistula

After extended periods of sample collection or the loss of a plug, the fistula may shrink to a size that prevents re-insertion of the normal plug. In such cases a smaller, cut-down plug is inserted and then the orifice slowly stretched over 2-3 days by insertion of spacers until the correct plug can be replaced. In severe cases local (spray) or even general anaesthetic may be needed to prevent the animal being subjected to undue discomfort. Indeed, in very extreme and persistent cases, surgical increase in the size of the fistula may be the best remedy.

Loss of rumen contents

Following the loss of the plug, continued rumination (for example, overnight) can result in almost total depletion of the animal's rumen contents, rumen stasis and inappetance. Restoration of ruminal activity can be achieved by taking part of the rumen contents from another OF or RF animal, and placing this into the rumen of the depleted animal through the oesophageal fistula. Additional salivary salts can be given in the same way.

Constant excessive leakage

Continued excessive salivary and rumen fluid loss will generally result in a fall in a condition of the animal, even when salivary salts are provided. This loss must be prevented by plug modifications. In less extreme cases one remedy is to fix a sponge tightly against the animal's neck around the plug. The offering of salivary salts in a liquid form as well as in general purpose salt blocks may also be necessary to restore electrolyte balance.

Abscess formation

This is quite common around the periphery of the fistula, especially at either end of the incision during the early post-operative period. Keeping the area clean and treating with antiseptic ointment normally proves effective. Systemic antibiotic treatment may be necessary in extreme cases. If similar abscesses occur during routine usage, collections should be stopped and treatment administered until healing is complete; the animal can then be used again normally.

3.9.3   Oesophageal Fistula Plugs

The plug can be made in moulded plastic or rubber or carved from a sheet of solid rubber. The dimensions vary with size, age and type of animal and are approximately 5 cm diameter for adult cattle and 3 cm diameter for calves and adult sheep.

Immediately after the operation to prepare the fistula the surrounding area may swell and it is advisable, expecially with cows and calves, to use a plug with a longer stem at this time. Once the swelling has subsided this should be replaced with a shorter-stemmed plug in order to reduce the weight and to reduce the danger of accidental extraction.

In manufacturing the plugs it is important that a smooth, round surface be produced. This is especially important where the stem joins the "wings" and at the tips of the "wings".

CHAPTER 4

ESTIMATING HERBAGE INTAKE FROM ANIMAL PERFORMANCE

R.D. Baker

4.1 INTRODUCTION

The use of animal performance data as a basis for calculating the herbage intake of grazing livestock is attractive because in its simplest form only the weighing of animal product, record keeping and calculations are involved. Thus the method offers an alternative to the more demanding techniques based upon pasture measurements or faecal output/digestibility relationships, in situations where labour and laboratory facilities are limiting.

Herbage intake (HI) is calculated from the energy requirements for the maintenance and production of the animals involved (E_{m+p}) and the total requirement equated with herbage of a given energy concentration (E_h). Thus:

$$HI = \frac{E_{m+p}}{E_h} \qquad (4.1)$$

The precision of the estimate is therefore entirely dependent on the adequacy of energy standards and the ability to measure animal production accurately. As with all techniques for estimating herbage intake there are errors and biases in the calculated figures arising from the assumptions made. The potential sources of variation are considered in the following sections.

4.2 MEASURES OF USABLE ENERGY

There is no common system of expressing the energy requirement of livestock or of evaluating the energy content of feeds. During the last few years a number of attempts have been made to improve existing systems and to develop new ones incorporating the findings arising from a better understanding of energy metabolism. Consequently, there are several measures and systems in operation and the choice of system can substantially affect the estimate of herbage intake under some circumstances.

Both energy values of feeds and animal requirements may be expressed in terms of Digestible Energy (DE), Metabolisable Energy (ME) or Net Energy (NE), as Total Digestible Nutrients (TDN) or as Feed Units.

All systems distinguish between dairy cows and growing/fattening cattle with the exception of the one adopted by the German Democratic Republic (Schiemann *et al*, 1971). There are, however, differences between systems because there is a lack of agreement on animal requirements, particularly for growing animals, and on the means of predicting the energy contents of feeds. There has also been a greater acceptance of simplification and the use of average figures in some schemes than others. For detailed descriptions the reader should refer to the National Research Council publications (1969; 1975; 1976; 1978) for the American TDN, DE, ME and NE systems, to MAFF (1975) and ARC (1980) for the British ME system and to Van Es (1978), Vermorel (1978), INRA (1978), Bickel and Landis (1978) and Bronsch *et al* (1979) for the NE systems adopted in Holland, France, Switzerland and West Germany respectively.

4.3 ENERGY REQUIREMENTS

4.3.1 **Maintenance**

It is generally accepted that maintenance requirements are proportional to some power of live weight and that they also depend on the extent of an animal's activity. The lack of agreement on whether the exponent should be liveweight $W^{0.75}$ or $W^{0.73}$ and on the additional energy requirements for activity will lead to variations in the estimates of herbage intake. In some cases maintenance is regarded as equal to fasting metabolism whereas in others an activity increment is added to allow for the energy expended for voluntary muscular activity associated with normal feeding conditions. Distinctions are drawn between tied animals (which sometimes are equated with those kept in calorimeters), loose housed animals and those grazing. Examples of the differences that arise for housed animals are given in Table 4.1.

Table 4.1 Requirements for maintenance expressed as net energy in relation to liveweight, (LW)

			Energy system			
	MAFF (1975)	NRC (1975, 1978)	Van Es (1978)	Vermorel (1978)	Bickel and Landis (1978)	Bronsch et al (1979)
Exponent of LW (e)	0.73	0.75	0.75	0.75	0.75	0.75
600 kg Cow						
Activity increment	+10%	+10%	0 (or +5%)	0 (or +10%)	0	0
Maintenance requirement MJ NE $kg^{-1}LW^e$	0.396	0.335	0.293 or (0.308)△	0.293 or (0.322)†	0.293	0.29
Total requirement MJ NE day^{-1}	42.2	40.6	35.5 (37.4)△	35.5 (39.1)†	35.5	35.5
250 kg Steer						
Activity increment	0	0	+10%	+10%	+10%	0
Maintenance requirement MJ NE $kg^{-1} LW^e$	0.396	0.322	0.330	0.333	0.330	0.293
Total requirement	21.1	20.2	20.7	20.7	20.7	18.4
60 kg Ewe						
Activity increment	+15%	NG	—	NG	—	—
Maintenance requirement MJ NE $kg^{-1} LW^e$	0.265	0.287§	—	0.278§	—	—
Total requirement MJ NE day^{-1}	5.3	6.2	—	6.0	—	—

NG = not stated whether an activity increment is included
△ = Requirement increased by 5% for loose housed cattle over tied cattle
† = Requirement increased by 10% for loose housed cattle over tied cattle
§ = Adjusted from ME with an efficiency of utilisation for maintenance of 0.70

The extent to which activity allowances should be increased for grazing animals cannot be stated with certainty. ARC (1965) concluded that estimates made of the energy cost of grazing do not warrant the inclusion of any additional allowance of the work of grazing but they did acknowledge the increased needs arising from extra walking, climbing or standing. Using their figures the 10% activity allowance recommended would be sufficient for cattle walking about 3 km daily.

The energy costs of horizontal movement by cattle and sheep have been stated as 2.0 and 2.6 J per kg LW per metre respectively (ARC, 1980). For vertical movement 28 J per kg LW per metre has been recommended for both cattle and sheep. The effect of a 400 kg bullock travelling 3 km and ascending 200 m daily is to increase energy expenditure by 4.64 MJ or 15 per cent in fasting metabolism. The increase for a 50 kg ewe would be 0.67 MJ or a 16% increase. No specific recommendation is made by MAFF (1975) but NRC (1978) recommended that maintenance for grazing dairy cows be increased by 3% for each km walked. They suggest that the needs are 10% higher for cows grazing lush pasture and as much as 20% for those grazing sparse pasture. The importance of the exercise factor in maintenance has been discussed by Logan and Pigden (1969) and the estimates made for the maintenance of sheep kept indoors and outdoors have been summarised by Tissier *et al* (1978). The average value for housed sheep was 0.397 MJ of ME per $W^{0.75}$ and this value had been adopted in the French system. Estimates for grazing sheep have ranged from 0.402 — 0.910 MJ ME with a mean value of 0.596 MJ per $W^{0.75}$, a 50% increase over housed sheep. All the latter estimates were made in New Zealand and Australia and their exact relevance to European conditions is uncertain.

The magnitude of the activity increment is the most important difficulty in estimating the maintenance requirements of grazing livestock. Also, small differences may arise, a) from fluctuations in gut fill which affect estimates of live weight, and b) from the effects of adverse weather conditions. Increases of up to 8% in total feed allowances have been recommended (NRC, 1978) for cows kept under severe winter conditions in the northern states of America. Precise estimates of maintenance energy requirements are generally not required for grazing livestock as controlled rationing of feed is normally not attempted. For this reason, and also because precise requirements are ill-defined, most of the energy systems adopted do not include guidance on the requirements of grazing animals. However, the evidence available indicates that 10-20% additional energy will be required by animals grazing small fields and paddocks but that substantially more will be required for those kept under hill and rangeland conditions.

4.3.2 **Milk production**

The net energy requirement for milk production is the energy value $(EV_L, MJ\ kg^{-1})$ of the milk secreted. This may be estimated for cows from the fat (BF), protein (P) and lactose (L) content $(g\ kg^{-1})$ or from fat and solids not fat (SNF) contents (Tyrell and Reid, 1965).

$$EV_L = 0.03840\ BF + 0.02226\ P + 0.01992\ L - 0.1081 \qquad (4.2)$$

or $\quad EV_L = 0.0386\ \ BF + 0.0205\ SNF - 0.236 \qquad (4.3)$

In some systems it is customary to relate requirements to 4% fat corrected milk (FCM) whereas others tabulate requirements against fat content or against fat and solids not fat contents. Solids corrected milk (SCM) may also be used. FCM and SCM can be calculated from the equations:

$$FCM = 0.4\ (weight\ of\ milk) + 15\ (weight\ of\ fat) \qquad (4.4)$$

$$SCM = Milk\ yield\ (kg) \times EV_L\ (MJ\ kg^{-1}) \div 3.1362\ (MJ\ kg^{-1}) \qquad (4.5)$$

The denominator in equation 4.5 is the approximate energy value of 1 kg 4% SCM. The actual values for FCM adopted by different countries vary in relation to what is considered the average milk produced. The range of values adopted, amounts to nearly 9% between NRC and the Netherlands, and is shown in Table 4.2.

Table 4.2   Energy values of 4% Fat Corrected Milk (MJ kg^{-1})

	Energy system					
	MAFF (1975)	NRC (1978)	Van Es (1978)	Vermorel (1978)	Bickel and Landis (1978)	Bronsch et al (1979)
Energy value (MJ/kg)	3.10	3.31	3.05	3.14	3.14	3.17

The requirements for net energy for the milk production of ewes is only stated in the British and French systems. A value of 4.6 MJ kg^{-1} has been adopted by the British and is also recommended by the French during the first month of lactation. During the second month a value of 4.4 MJ is taken. An alternative approach for ewes has also been given by Brett *et al* (1972) who estimated energy value (MJ kg^{-1}) by regression on the days (D) after lambing, where BF is g kg^{-1}.

$$EV_L = 0.0328\ BF + 0.025\ D + 2.203 \qquad (4.6)$$

4.3.3 **Pregnancy**

Pregnant animals have a higher basal metabolism and require additional energy to cover this need and for the synthesis of foetal and associated tissues and their maintenance. The foetus, foetal membranes, fluids and the uterus grow at an exponential rate. Thus some 64% (Becker *et al*, 1950) of the total foetus and accompanying tissue and fluids were laid down in Jersey cows in the last 2 months of pregnancy and 70% in Merino ewes carrying a single foetus over the same period (Langlands and Sutherland, 1968). For the most part the extra requirements for pregnancy are ignored during the first 6 to 7 months of gestation for cattle and the first 90 days for sheep. However, MAFF (1975) have published equations which allow pregnancy needs to be calculated throughout gestation for cattle and over the last 8 weeks of pregnancy for single and twin bearing ewes. For cows the energy requirement will have already increased by about 13% after 6 months but only by 3-5 % for ewes after 90 days. A more recent assessment of data (ARC, 1980) indicates that these equations are outdated, and new equations are given which permit the calculation of energy retention in the foetus and gravid uterus for cattle and sheep in relation to stage of gestation and the expected birth weight. During the final month the suggested requirements are 100 per cent greater for cattle and 10-20% greater for sheep than MAFF (1975).

Precise requirements for pregnancy are not stated in all feeding systems and, as for maintenance and lactation, there is no universal agreement on them. For cows the requirement for the seventh month of pregnancy is generally stated as the equivalent of approximately 2 kg FCM but ranges from 4 to 8 kg in the ninth month depending on the feeding standards adopted. Variations also exist in the standards adopted for ewes. For example, the MAFF and French standards suggest that the energy requirement during the last six weeks of pregnancy is about 1.3 and 1.5 x maintenance for single and twin bearing 60 kg ewes whereas the NRC standards are 1.5 and 2.0 x maintenance. New standards suggested by ARC (1980) are similar to the latter at 1.5 and 1.8 x maintenance.

4.3.4 **Liveweight gain or loss**

The energy requirements for liveweight gain increase with the growth of young animals but remain relatively constant for mature adults. They are also influenced markedly by the rate of gain or animal production level (APL) and the energy concentration of the food. The current feeding standards are mainly based on a variable Net Energy system, which was developed from the principles established by MacHardy (1966) and worked out in detail by Harkins *et al* (1974). This approach enables tables to be constructed which allow the net energy values (NE_{mp}) to be obtained if the animal production level (n times maintenance) and the energy value of the foods are known.

Although most systems for expressing requirements have a common basis there are still substantial differences in the values adopted. These relate both to maintenance and production requirements. For example, MAFF (1975) recognise that the efficiency of utilisation of ME for maintenance (k_m) varies with the energy concentration of the diet but, because in practice dietary extremes are found infrequently, they adopt single values for cattle and sheep of 0.72 and 0.70 respectively. However, the Dutch vary the k_m of cattle from 0.68 — 0.75 over the range of dietary energy concentrations of 8-14 M/D, and NRC (1976) by 0.58 — 0.69 over the same range. Thus, although the net energy requirements in the three systems are almost identical, when expressed as ME for maintenance of grazing cattle consuming grass with an M/D of 11, the calculated requirement by NRC is 13% higher.

The daily metabolisable energy requirement is computed from the energy value of the gain and efficiency of ME utilisation for gain (k_f). As before, the k_f values are related to the energy concentration of the foods and those adopted by NRC (1976) are about 10% units lower than those adopted in Europe.

A more serious potential source of error in attempting to estimate herbage intake from records of liveweight gain arises from the failure of most feeding standards to take into account the effect of breed, sex and previous nutrition on the quantity of energy deposited per kg liveweight. Estimates for animals of the same liveweight and growing at the same rate vary by anything up to 100% (Van Es, 1978). Thus reasonably accurate estimates of herbage intake will be possible only when the energy requirements used in the calculations reflect the breed and sex of the animals used. There are varying degrees of sophistication in the approaches adopted. The French and ARC (1980) systems take account of differences between bulls, steers and heifers, as well as the rate of maturity of breeds. In contrast the MAFF scheme gives general tables applicable to all cattle. The same considerations apply in estimating the herbage intake of sheep but as with cattle a knowledge of the energy values of the liveweight gain is necessary before they can be taken into account.

Animals, particularly those lactating, may also go through periods of liveweight loss, and adjustments are required to estimate requirements to take account of this source of energy. The average value of body tissue energy for cows has been taken as 20 MJ (MAFF, 1975), 21 MJ (Van Es, 1978) or 25 MJ per kg liveweight (NRC, 1978; Vermorel, 1978). It has been assumed that it is used with an efficiency of 0.82 for lactation and that its equivalence in dietary ME can be obtained by dividing by the feed k_1 (0.62) for lactation to give a value of 26.5 MJ kg^{-1} (MAFF, 1975). No comparable figures for sheep were recommended. However, Robinson (1978) has suggested a figure of 25 MJ kg^{-1} liveweight. More recently ARC (1980) have reviewed available information on the energy content of liveweight for cattle and sheep and suggest the adoption of a single value of 26 MJ kg^{-1}. Thus, its equivalence in dietary energy would be 34 MJ kg^{-1}.

4.4 THE ENERGY VALUE OF HERBAGE

Before herbage intakes can be calculated from the estimated energy requirements of animals an assessment of the energy value of the herbage is necessary. In some cases suitable values chosen from tables of feed composition will be adequate. When greater precision is required it will be necessary to obtain samples of the herbage being eaten and to subject them to chemical analysis. Samples of herbage may be obtained by the use of oesophageal fistulated animals but if these are not available some other method of estimating the composition of the diet will be more appropriate. Normally samples would be collected by hand, taking care to ensure they are representative of the herbage being selected (see Chapter 3).

The energy values of forages have been determined directly from controlled feeding trials to establish digestibility or Total Digestible Nutrients; from gross energy determinations on feeds and faeces to determine Metabolisable Energy (having assumed a loss of methane energy and either assumed or measured a loss of urine energy); or from calorimetric studies to extend the evaluation to Net Energy by direct determinations of methane output and heat production. From the information gathered on feeds many prediction equations have been developed linking digestibility and chemical composition to the metabolisable value of the feed. The equations adopted reflect the type of information available on feeds within a country and the choice of energy system.

One of the most comprehensive sets of data on fresh forages has been collected by Terry *et al* (1973) who related digestible energy (DE) to the contents (g kg^{-1}DM) of crude protein (CP) and digestible organic matter in the dry matter (D) by the equation:

$$DE = 0.1233\ CP + 0.1705\ D + 0.285\ \text{MJ kg}^{-1}\text{DM}$$
$$\text{and ME assumed} = 0.815 \times DE \tag{4.7}$$

Other equations are based mainly on either total or digestible contents of crude protein, crude fat (CL), crude fibre (CF) and N-free extract (NFE).

The calculated intake of herbage will vary depending on which equation is used to predict energy value. Besides differences in the coefficient established, the need for separate constants to deal with differences between the value of forage for cattle and sheep is recognised in some equations and adjustments for level of feeding may also be incorporated. A comparison of the "energy potential" of feeds is given in Table 4.3 for two fresh grasses given by MAFF (1975).

Table 4.3   The estimated metabolisable energy value of fresh permanent pasture grass

	Prediction equation						
	MAFF (1975)	Terry et al (1973)	NRC (1969)	Van Es (1978)	Vermorel (1978)	Bickel and Landis (1978)	Bronsch et al (1978)
Pasture grass closely grazed non-rotational	12.1	13.3	12.0	12.0(C) 12.1(S)	12.0(C) 12.1(S)	12.0	12.1(C) 12.4(S)
Rotational with monthly intervals	11.2	12.0	11.3	11.1(C) 11.2(S)	11.2(C) 11.3(S)	10.9	11.1(C) 11.3(S)

(C) = cattle, (S) = sheep
Based upon closely grazed, pasture grass having CP, CL, CF and NFE contents of 265, 55, 130 and 455 g kg^{-1}DM and digestible contents of 225, 35, 105 and 387 g respectively: and grass grazed rotationally having contents of 175, 50, 225 and 460 g kg^{-1}DM and digestible contents of 130, 25, 185 and 377 g respectively.

4.5 MEASURING ANIMAL PRODUCTION

The measurement of the milk production and milk quality of dairy cows can be done simply and accurately provided accepted procedures are followed. For example, recording the milk yield and taking aliquot samples for milk analysis at each milking on 1-2 days each week. However, for beef cows and ewes the task is more difficult. There are four main approaches to the problem of milk yield estimation and the reader should refer to Corbett (1978) for a general consideration of the different approaches. They are:

1. Weighing of offspring before and after a number of consecutive sucklings.
2. Measurement of milk secretion rate over periods of 4-8 hours.
3. Estimation from previously established regression equations between liveweight gain and milk composition.
4. Estimates made from water turnover in the offspring.

Further information on the relative merits of the suckling and machine milking techniques has recently become available (Le Du *et al*, 1979; Doney *et al*, 1979; Somerville and Lowman, 1980) and on the estimation of milk quality following removal of milk after oxytocin injections (Le Du *et al*, 1978).

The accurate estimation of liveweight change is of major importance if

good estimates of herbage intake are to be obtained. Errors and possible
bias in the estimates readily arise from changes in gut fill and the
replacement of fat by water in animals losing weight. A further problem
arises because the composition of the gain will vary in relation to breed, sex,
age and, in some circumstances, previous nutrition. Also, over short periods
of time recorded liveweight gains and losses can be quite meaningless even
when there is strict control over gut fill changes. Therefore estimates of
energy loss or storage tend to become more accurate the longer the
recording period; usually periods of less than 4-6 weeks are unsatisfactory.
The difficulties of making measurements of liveweight and body
composition and the precautions necessary have also been outlined by
Corbett (1978) who also makes references to the more detailed
investigations upon which recommendations are made.

A further complication arises for pregnant animals as it is necessary to
distinguish between liveweight gains due to increases in the weight of the
foetus and accompanying tissues and fluids, and those that are a genuine
change in the body tissues of the dam. This is of importance because the
energy value of the liveweight increase arising from the gravid uterus of both
cattle and sheep is less than 5MJ kg^{-1}, until the last month of pregnancy.
Equations to predict the liveweight changes associated with pregnancy and
their energy contents have been published by ARC (1980) and calculated
values for cattle and sheep carrying different foetal burdens are given in
Tables 4.4 and 4.5 respectively.

Table 4.4 Estimated daily weight changes for the gravid uterus of cattle at 4 weekly intervals from conception (kg)

| | Total foetal weight at birth (kg) | | | |
	25	35	45	55
Days from conception				
113–141	0.13	0.15	0.18	0.20
142–169	0.16	0.21	0.26	0.31
170–197	0.21	0.29	0.36	0.44
198–225	0.26	0.37	0.49	0.60
226–253	0.32	0.47	0.63	0.78
254–281	0.38	0.56	0.76	0.97

Derived from equation given by ARC (1980)

Table 4.5 Estimated daily weight changes for the gravid uterus of sheep at 4 weekly intervals from conception (g)

	Total foetal weight at birth (kg)			
	4	6	8	10
Days from conception				
63 – 91	30	46	57	69
92 – 119	59	92	115	144
120 – 147	96	140	205	260

Derived from equation given by ARC (1980)

4.6 STANDARDS FOR THE CALCULATION OF ENERGY OUTPUT AND HERBAGE INTAKE

The calculation of herbage intake can be undertaken from a detailed consideration of maintenance, activity and production requirements, from the efficiencies of conversion associated with each of these processes, and from herbage analysis. For such an exercise individual judgements must be made on how appropriate each source of data is to the circumstances for which a calculation is being made. The most up-to-date collations of information are INRA (1978) and ARC (1980).

Normally, recommended standards for energy requirements and the energy value of forages will be used and, as an example, those published by MAFF (1975) are given. In these recommendations it is suggested that the energy requirement for fasting metabolism should be increased by 15% to cover the extra maintenance costs of sheep kept outdoors, and there is a 5% safety margin included in all values. No specific recommendation is made for cattle kept outdoors, but the recommended allowances besides having the usual safety margin also include a 10% activity increment. In other systems safety allowances *per se* are not incorporated into the recommendations. The effect of doing so in the MAFF system is to increase requirements for most productive animals by some 5-15% over maintenance. This addition coupled with the 10% activity increment is therefore similar to that recommended by NRC for good pasture conditions and the direct application of MAFF standards in these circumstances is likely to be appropriate.

The recommended requirements (MAFF, 1975) for livestock are given below.

4.6.1   Dairy and Beef cows

ME allowance for maintenance (MJ day^{-1})

$E_m = 8.3 + 0.091$ W where W = liveweight (kg)   (4.8)

ME allowance for milk production (MJ day^{-1})

$E_l = 4.94$ Y where Y = milk yield of average quality (kg day^{-1})   (4.9)

or $E_l = \dfrac{\text{Energy secreted as milk (EV}_1) \times \text{Y}}{\text{Efficiency of energy utilisation for lactation (k}_l)}$ (4.10)

$EV_1 = 0.0386$ BF $+ 0.0205$ SNF $- 0.236$ (MJ day^{-1})   (4.11)

$k_l = 0.62$ (4.12)

ME allowance for pregnancy (MJ day^{-1})

$E_{preg} = 1.13 \, e^{0.0106t}$ where t = number of days pregnant and   (4.13)
$\qquad\qquad\qquad\qquad$ e = 2.718 the base of the natural logarithm

ME allowance for liveweight gain

$E_g = +34$ MJ kg^{-1} gain   (4.14)

ME allowance for liveweight loss

$E_g = -28$ MJ kg^{-1} loss   (4.15)

As with all recommended allowances a 5% safety margin has been added to the figure for liveweight loss. The justification for its inclusion as additional energy being available to the animal has not been given. As a safety margin to prevent the loss being over-valued a 5% deduction would be more logical. An unadjusted figure of 26.5 MJ is perhaps more appropriate to grazing cows when their herbage consumption is being estimated.

4.6.2   Growing cattle

ME allowance for maintenance (MJ day^{-1})

$E_m = 8.3 + 0.091$ W where W = liveweight (kg)   (4.16)

ME allowance for growth (MJ day^{-1})

ME for production = $\dfrac{\text{Net energy stored (E}_g)}{\text{Efficiency of ME utilisation for gain (k}_f)}$ (4.17)

$$E_g = 1.05 \left[\frac{\text{LWG } (6.28 + 0.0188 \text{ W})}{(1 - 0.3 \text{ LWG})} \right] \begin{array}{l}\text{where LWG} = \text{daily} \\ \text{liveweight gain (kg)}\end{array} \quad (4.18)$$

$K_f = 0.0414$ M/D $\hspace{4cm}$ (4.19)
M/D = ME concentration of dry matter (MJ day^{-1})

4.6.3 Ewes

ME allowance for maintenance (MJ day^{-1})

$E_m = 1.8 + 0.1$ W $\hspace{5cm}$ (4.20)

ME allowance for milk production (MJ day^{-1})

$E_p = 7.8$ Y where Y = milk yield (kg day^{-1}) $\hspace{2cm}$ (4.21)

ME required for maintenance and pregnancy (MJ day^{-1})

For ewes with single lambs $E_{mp} = (1.2 + 1.05 \text{ w}) \, e^{0.0072t}$ $\hspace{0.5cm}$ (4.22)

For ewes with twin lambs $E_{mp} = (0.8 + 0.04 \text{ W}) \, e^{0.0105t}$ $\hspace{0.5cm}$ (4.23)
$\hspace{4cm}$ where t = number of days pregnant

NB. These equations only apply to the last 8 weeks of pregnancy.

ME allowances for liveweight gain

$E_g = 42$ MJ kg^{-1} gain (calculated from Robinson, 1978 with a $\hspace{0.3cm}$ (4.24)
$\hspace{3cm}$ 5% safety margin)

ME allowance for liveweight loss

$E_g = -33$ MJ kg^{-1} loss (calculated from Robinson, 1978 with $\hspace{0.2cm}$ (4.25)
$\hspace{3cm}$ no safety margin)

4.6.4 Growing sheep

ME allowance for maintenance (MJ day^{-1})

$E_m = 1.4 + 0.15$ W where W = liveweight (kg) $\hspace{1.5cm}$ (4.26)

ME allowance for growth (MJ day^{-1})

$$\text{ME for production} = \frac{\text{Net energy stored } (E_g)}{\text{Efficiency of ME utilisation for gain } (k_f)} \quad (4.27)$$

$E_g = \text{antilog} \, [1.11 \log_{10} \text{LWG} + 0.004 \text{ W} - 2.10]$
where LWG = daily liveweight gain (g) $\hspace{3cm}$ (4.28)

$k_f = 0.0435$ M/D

M/D = ME concentration of dry matter (MJ kg^{-1})   (4.29)

4.6.5 Deductions for supplementary feeds

Milk. In assessing the intake of suckling animals a deduction has to be made for the quantity of milk consumed. The energy values of average milk are for cows, 2.92 and for ewes, 4.60 MJ kg^{-1}. The apparent digestibility of milk is 98% and its ME = 97% of DE (Jagusch, 1968). Consequently the contribution of milk to energy requirements is:

Cows $0.98 \times 0.97 \times 2.92 = 2.78$ MJ kg^{-1} Milk   (4.30)

Ewes $0.98 \times 0.97 \times 4.60 = 4.37$ MJ kg^{-1} Milk   (4.31)

Concentrates and forage supplements. When supplementary feeds are given at pasture it is also necessary to make a deduction for their energy contribution. Feeds are credited with their stated ME value and it is assumed that there is no associative effect of feeds on their ME values. Supplementation will normally increase the level of feeding and in doing so may lead to a level of feeding effect on digestibility. The possibility of such an effect occurring is not acknowledged in the MAFF (1975) system and could lead to a bias in the estimate of herbage intake (see Chapter 3).

4.7 THE ACCURACY OF ESTIMATING HERBAGE INTAKE FROM ANIMAL PERFORMANCE

In the foregoing sections some of the variations that exist in the energy values adopted for the requirements of cattle and sheep and feeds have been highlighted. In some instances, these are of such a magnitude that the estimates of herbage intake from animal production data may be subject to large errors. In practice, however, the calculation is likely to be used most frequently to give an indirect estimate of the relative removal of herbage from a pasture by one grazing treatment compared with one or more other treatments. The errors involved will tend to be systematic and in the same direction for each treatment. However, this is not the case if level of feeding effects occur.

Despite all the potential inaccuracies of the technique it has been found useful for obtaining relative measures of herbage intake, pasture productivity and the contribution of herbage to the diet of grazed animals; the last two providing measures of performance which have proved useful indicators of the efficiency with which grassland is utilised. The accuracy with which estimates of herbage intake can be made from measures of animal production cannot be stated precisely. However, for the most part, differences in the standards adopted for maintenance and production are unlikely to bias calculations by more than 10 per cent, a variability no greater than that of the alternative techniques. More difficult to assess is the impact of being unable to take account of any increases in energy requirements associated with the process of grazing. These can be considerable under extensive and adverse grazing conditions but may be of only minor consequence when adequate, high quality herbage is available. Provided animal production is assessed accurately the system outlined will provide estimates of herbage intake which are acceptable for many purposes but it is not a method that can be recommended for critical studies, particularly over short time periods because of the difficulties of accurately estimating changes in body weight. As new information becomes available, the standards adopted will inevitably be modified to take account of it but the approach to the calculation of herbage intake will remain unchanged. In the following example calculations the standards currently recommended for Britain (MAFF, 1975) have been used.

4.7.1 Example calculations

Examples of herbage intake calculations from animal performance are given below for lactating dairy cows, steers, ewes and lambs.

4.7.1.1 *600 kg Cows giving 25, 17 or 12 kg milk daily at different stages of gestation, Group A receiving 2 kg supplementary feed*

	A	B	C
Milk, kg day^{-1}	25	17	12
Liveweight change, kg day^{-1}	-0.25	0	0.25
Days of gestation (t)	0	90	180
Maintenance $= 8.3 + 0.091 (600)$	62.9	62.9	62.9
Liveweight loss $= 0.25 \times 26.5$	-6.6	—	—
Liveweight gain $= 0.25 \times 34$	—	—	8.5
Pregnancy gain $= 1.13\, e^{0.0106t}$	—	2.9	7.6
Milk $= 4.94 \times$ yield	123.5	84.0	59.3
Total requirement, MJ day^{-1}	179.8	149.8	138.3
Supplementary concentrate, A $= 2$ kg day at 11.5 ME kg^{-1}	-23.0	—	—
Total energy from grass	156.8	149.8	138.3
Calculated herbage intake (kg DM day^{-1}) at grass M/D of 11 $=$	14.3	13.6	12.6

4.7.1.2 *200 kg steers gaining 0.9 kg daily and receiving no additional feed (A) or 7 kg milk (B)*

	A	B
Maintenance 8.3 × 0.91 (200)	26.5	26.5

Liveweight gain

$$E_g = 1.05 \frac{0.9\,(6.28 + 0.0188 \times 200)}{1 - 0.3\,(0.9)} \div k_f$$

	A	B
Grass M/D = 11, therefore k_f = 0.0414 × 11 = 0.455	28.6	
or assumed M/D for mixed diet of 14, k_f = 0.58		22.4
Milk contribution 7 × 2.78	—	−19.5
Total requirement, MJ day⁻¹	55.1	29.4
Calculated herbage intake (kg DM day⁻¹) at grass		
M/D of 11 =	5.0	2.7

4.7.1.3 *A 60 kg ewe giving 2 kg milk daily and gaining 50 g day⁻¹*

Maintenance = 1.8 + 0.1 (60)	7.8
Milk = 2 × 7.8	15.6

Liveweight gain
$$E_g = \text{antilog } 1.11 \log_{10} 50 + (0.004 \times 60) - 2.10 \div k_f$$
$$k_f = 0.0435 \times 11 = 0.479$$

	2.2
Total requirements, MJ day⁻¹	24.6
Calculated herbage intake (kg DM day⁻¹) at grass M/D of 11 =	2.2

4.7.1.4 *A 30 kg lamb growing at 200 g day⁻¹ and receiving 750 g day⁻¹ of milk*

Maintenance = 1.4 + 0.15 (30)	5.9

Liveweight gain
$$E_g \text{ antilog } 1.11 \log_{10} 200 + (0.004 \times 30) - 2.10 \div k_f$$

Estimated M/D of diet = 13.6 giving a k_f of 0.592	6.3
Milk contribution 0.7 × 4.37	−3.3
Total requirement	8.9
Calculated herbage intake (g DM day⁻¹) at grass M/D of 11 =	809

4.8 REFERENCES

AGRICULTURAL RESEARCH COUNCIL (ARC), (1965). *Nutrient Requirements of Farm Livestock* No. 2. Ruminants, ARC, London, pp 264.

AGRICULTURAL RESEARCH COUNCIL (ARC), (1980). *The Nutrient Requirements of Ruminant Livestock.* Commonwealth Agricultural Bureaux, Farnham Royal, pp 351.

BECKER, R B, DIX ARNOLD, P T and MARSHALL, S P (1950). Changes in weight of the reproductive organs of the dairy cow and their relation to long-term feeding investigations. *Journal of Dairy Science,*

33, 911-917.

BICKEL, H and LANDIS, J (1978). Feed evaluation for ruminants. 3. Proposed application of the new system of energy evaluation in Switzerland. *Livestock Production Science*, 5, 367-372.

BRETT, D J, CORBETT, J L and INSKIP, M W (1972). Estimation of the energy value of ewe milk. *Proceedings of the Australian Society of Animal Production*, 9, 286-291.

BRONSCH, K, FREESE, H H, HAGEMEISTER, H, KAUFMANN, W, KIRCHGESSNER, M, MENKE, K H, OSLAGE, H J, ROHR, K and VOGT, H (1979). Nettoenergie-Laktation (NEL) — die neue energetische futterbewertung für milchkühe. *Deutsche Landwistshafts-Gesellshaft-Mitterlungen*, Heft 11, 7, 672.

CORBETT, J L (1978). Measuring sward performance. In: L't Mannetje (ed) "*Measurement of Grassland Vegetation and Production*", Commonwealth Agricultural Bureaux, Farnham Royal, pp 163-231.

DONEY, J M, PEART, J N, SMITH, W F and LAUDA, F (1979). A consideration of the techniques for estimation of milk yield by suckled sheep and a comparison of estimates obtained by two methods in relation to effect of breed, level of production and stage of lactation. *Journal of Agricultural Science, Cambridge*, 92, 123-132.

HARKINS, J, EDWARDS, R A and McDONALD, P (1974). A new net-energy system for ruminants. *Animal Production*, 19, 141-148.

INRA (1978). *Alimentation des Ruminants*. Ed INRA Publications, 78000 Versailles.

JAGUSCH, K T (1968). *The utilization of energy by milk-fed lambs with special reference to the composition of the gain*. PhD Thesis, University of Sydney.

LANGLANDS, J P and SUTHERLAND, H A M (1968). An estimate of the nutrients utilized for pregnancy by Merino sheep. *British Journal of Nutrition*, 22, 217-227.

LE DU, Y L P, BAKER, R D and BARKER, J M (1978). The use of short term secretion rate measurements for estimating the milk production of suckler cows. *Journal of Dairy Research*, 45, 1-4.

LE DU, Y L P, MACDONALD, A J and PEART, J N (1979). Comparison of two techniques for estimating the milk production of suckled cows. *Livestock Production Science*, 6, 277-281.

LOGAN, V S and PIGDEN, W J (1969). Estimating herbage yield from energy intake of grazing ruminants. Experimental Methods for Evaluating Herbage. *Publication 1315, Canadian Department of Agriculture*, pp 223.

MacHARDY, F V (1966). Simplified ratio formulation. *9th International Congress of Animal Production*, Edinburgh p 25, Oliver and Boyd, Edinburgh.

MINISTRY OF AGRICULTURE, FISHERIES AND FOOD (1975). Energy allowances and feeding systems for ruminants. *Technical Bulletin 33, London, HMSO*.

NATIONAL RESEARCH COUNCIL (NRC), (1969). *United States-Canadian Tables of Feed Composition*. National Academy of Sciences, Washington, DC.

NATIONAL RESEARCH COUNCIL (NRC), (1975). "*Nutrient Requirements of Sheep*" 5th revised edition, National Academy of Sciences, Washington, DC.

NATIONAL RESEARCH COUNCIL (NRC), (1976). "*Nutrient Requirements of Beef Cattle*" 5th revised edition, National Academy of Science, Washington, DC.

NATIONAL RESEARCH COUNCIL (NRC), (1978). "*Nutrient Requirements of Dairy Cattle*" 5th revised edition, National Academy of Sciences, Washington, DC.

ROBINSON, J J (1978). Milk production in the ewe. *European Association of Animal Production, Publication No 23*.

SCHIEMANN, R, NEHRING, K, HOFFMANN, L. JENTSCH, W and CHUDY, A. (1971). *Energetische Futterbewertung und Energienormen*. VEB Deutscher Landwirstshafteverlog, Berlin, 344 pp.

SOMERVILLE, S H and LOWMAN, B G (1980). A comparison of machine-milking and the calf-suckling technique as methods of measuring the milk yield of beef cows. *Animal Production*, 30, 365-372.

TERRY, R A, OSBOURN, D F, CAMMELL, S B and FENLON, J S (1973). *In vitro* digestibility and the estimation of energy in herbage. *Proceedings of the 5th General Meeting, European Grassland Federation, Uppsala, Sweden*, Vaxtodling 28, pp 19-25.

TISSIER, M, THERIEZ, M, GUEGUEN, L and MOLENAT, G (1978). Ovine, in INRA 1978 *Alimentation des Ruminants* Ed INRA Publications, Versailles, pp 597.

TYRELL, H F and REID, J T (1965). Prediction of energy value of cows milk. *Journal of Dairy Science*, 48, 1215-1223.

VAN ES, A J H (1978). Feed evaluation for ruminants. 1. The system in use from May 1977 in the Netherlands. *Livestock Production Science*, 5, 331-345.

VERMOREL, M (1978). Feed evaluation for ruminants. 2. The new energy systems proposed in France. *Livestock Production Science*, 5, 347-365.

CHAPTER 5

MEASUREMENT OF HERBAGE INTAKE BY HOUSED ANIMALS

M. Chenost and C. Demarquilly

5.1 INTRODUCTION

Measurement of the amount of fresh herbage eaten by housed (zero grazed) animals may have various objectives:

(i) to study systematically the effect of 'physiological' changes with age of plants during successive growth cycles, and of environmental factors on the intake of the main herbage species. This type of study is usually carried out in conjunction with a measure of digestibility.

(ii) to study intake changes following various methods of conservation by measuring the amount of herbage/forage consumed before and after conservation.

(iii) to study intake differences between plants of different varieties or species particularly for plant breeding purposes.

(vi) to estimate the amount of herbage consumed by the productive animal zero grazed in the summer, to specify the quantity and quality of supplement required to meet production targets.

(v) to estimate the herbage intake of the grazing animal and the factors influencing that intake. It is simpler and more precise to measure this for housed animals than for those grazing at pasture.

In this chapter the methods of cutting and feeding cut herbage, the experimental constraints, and the value of this indirect evaluation of intake compared with animals grazing the same grass in the field are discussed. For specific technical aspects (materials, equipment, experimental procedures) see publications by the following authors (Minson *et al*, 1976; Heaney *et al*, 1968; Cammell, 1977; Zemmelink, 1980).

5.2 MEASUREMENT OF THE AMOUNT CONSUMED

Whatever the objective in measuring herbage intake it is important to know to what extent conditions of harvesting or conditioning, and methods of feeding affect the amount consumed indoors and whether the results can be transposed to other animals.

5.2.1 Harvesting and conditioning of herbage

The following factors can influence the amount of harvested herbage consumed:
— type of presentation (long, lacerated or chopped)
— height of cut
— previous management of the pasture (cut or grazed)
— frequency of cutting, duration and method of storage of grass between harvesting and feeding

5.2.1.1 *Harvesting machinery*. Herbage cut with a finger bar mower and harvested in the long form, can be picked up either manually with a fork or mechanically by the pick-up of a self-loading trailer. More commonly, herbage is harvested with the following types of forage harvester:
— flail type, which lacerates and breaks down the forage into lengths of 10-20 cm
— double chop, which gives a shorter chop of 5-15 cm
— precision chop, which produces forage of 0.5-5 cm lengths depending on the setting of the machine

Chopped versus long herbage
In an experiment with sheep, Dulphy (unpublished) offered first growth tall fescue either unchopped (cut with a mower and picked up with a fork) or chopped (2-4 cm long using a chaff cutter). The dry matter intake by two groups of six sheep are shown in Table 5.1. Chopping slightly increased the amount eaten, the animals spending slightly longer feeding on the chopped forage (15-20 min d^{-1}) and having a greater rate of intake.

Chopped versus lacerated herbage
Tayler and Rudman (1965) studied the amount consumed and the

performance of steers fed on the same forages either harvested with a flail type harvester or cut with a finger bar mower and picked up with a chopper type forage harvester. The animals fed on chopped grass consumed slightly more dry matter than those fed on lacerated grass (Table 5.2). The authors showed that the differences were more important with mature forage because the flail type harvester mixed the dead parts of the plant with the green parts making selection by the animal more difficult.

Table 5.1   Effect of chopping on the amount of first growth tall fescue eaten by sheep (Dulphy, unpublished)

| | DM intake g/kg $W^{0.75}$ | |
	Long	Chopped
Pre-heading	57.7 (100)	61.4 (106)
Heading	50.3 (100)	54.6 (109)

Table 5.2   Effect of method of harvesting on the herbage consumption of steers (Tayler and Rudman, 1965)

| | Flail forage harvester | Mower and chopper blower |
	DM intake (kg day^{-1})	
Forage harvested		
in spring	4.81 (100)	4.94 (103)
in summer	5.58 (100)	5.95 (107)

Table 5.3   Effects of method of harvesting and previous grazing on herbage consumption by steers (Tayler and Rudman, 1965)

| | Flail forage harvester | Mower and chopper blower |
	DM intake (kg day^{-1})	
Sward previously cut	6.26 (100)	6.38 (102)
Sward previously grazed	3.59 (100)	4.76 (133)

The same authors found that the effect of laceration was even more marked when the forage was harvested from a sward previously grazed (Table 5.3). On average the liveweight gains of the steers were from 3 to 25% lower with the lacerated grass than with the grass mown and then chopped. This decrease in the intake of lacerated forage, which can have a marked effect on the performance of the animals, was also found by Michalet-Doreau and Dulphy (unpublished) with dry ewes fed on a 3rd cut of Italian ryegrass either lacerated (flail type harvester) or chopped (precision chop harvester), the decrease being 13%.

Indirect evidence of the influence of type of forage harvester on herbage intake was also found by Demarquilly (1970) when studying the artificial drying of forage. The intake of dehydrated grasses harvested with a flail type harvester was lower (15.4%) than the intake of corresponding green forage (cut with a motor mower and then chopped into lengths of 2-4 cm with a chaff cutter). In contrast the intake of dehydrated grasses harvested with a double chop or precision chop harvester was slightly higher (3.4%) than the intake of the corresponding green forages.

It can be concluded from these studies that the form of presentation (long, chopped or lacerated) affects the amount of fresh herbage consumed by ruminants, and consequently affects their performance. The presentation which gives the greatest intake seems to be herbage, chopped into lengths of 2-4 cm. Chopping limits selection by the animals, in particular by sheep and goats fed indoors, so that the composition and digestibility of the herbage consumed are very similar to that offered, at least when the proportion of refusals allowed is limited (c 10%). When studying the influence of conservation on intake of forages, it is preferable that the green forage fed indoors and the conserved forage, are harvested with the same machine and cut at the same height.

5.2.1.2   *Cutting height.* Harvesters normally cut the grass at a height of 5-7 cm above ground level, but the cutting height can vary considerably depending on the setting of the machine. There is only limited evidence available, however, on the influence of height of cutting on amount of grass consumed.

Table 5.4   *Effect of method of harvesting fresh herbage on the liveweight gain (kg day^{-1}) of steers (Tayler and Rudman, 1965)*

	Mower and chopper blower	Forage harvester
Cut at 10 cm above ground	0.91	0.84
Cut at 6.5 cm above ground	0.81	0.71

Table 5.5   *Effect of fraction of sward on liveweight gain (kg day^{-1}) of steers (Tayler and Rudman, 1965)*

	Top fraction	Bottom fraction
Spring	0.89	0.58
Summer	0.74	0.64

Tayler and Rudman (1965) compared the growth rates of steers offered grass cut at 6.5 to 10 cm above ground level, either with a finger bar mower and then picked up with a chopper type harvester, or with a flail type harvester (Table 5.4). The lower cut (6.5 cm) gave slightly lower animal performance. Differences in performance were more marked (Table 5.5) when the animals were offered either the top fraction of the sward (cut at 13.5 cm above ground level), or the bottom fraction (the remainder cut at 6.5 cm). As the digestibility measured *in vitro*, was practically the same for top and bottom fractions in these experiments, the observed differences must be attributed to the amounts consumed. The authors were able to explain the reduced intakes by differences in the morphological characteristics of the forage (smaller proportion of leaves), the greater proportion of weeds and debris and a higher level of rust infection in the bottom fraction. In many cases, contamination of forage by soil would also occur, particularly when a cut is taken close to ground level.

Although the effect of height of cutting on amounts consumed has not been fully quantified, it is important that the cut should be taken at the same height when comparing intakes of a conserved forage to that of standing green forage. The cut should also be taken at the height of the stubble left after grazing by cattle, when the intake of grazed grass has to be estimated.

5.2.1.3 *Influence of previous grazing.* Palatability of grass can be affected by animal excreta from the previous use of the pasture. Animals in pens cannot eat as selectively as grazing animals and this significantly lowers their intake compared with grazing animals. This has been noted by several authors (Hutton, 1962; Demarquilly, 1966; Chenost and Demarquilly, 1969; Tayler and Rudman, 1965). Tayler and Rudman (Table 5.3) observed a significant decrease in the amounts of grass consumed when it was harvested from a field previously grazed compared with a field previously cut; the decrease being 25% for grass harvested by finger bar mower and 43% for grass harvested by flail type harvester. In a trial with dairy cows (Demarquilly, 1966), the decrease was on average 42% when the grass was cut with a finger bar mower and manually harvested with a fork.

Therefore it would appear that estimates of the intake of a crop harvested from a previously grazed field may give a considerable under-estimation of the intake of this herbage grazed "in situ".

5.2.1.4 *Effect of cutting frequency.* Studies carried out at the Grassland Research Institute, Hurley, show that herbage cut once daily can satisfactorily be fed in one or two feeds per day (Grassland Research Institute, 1966). Studies in Ireland (Collins, 1973) have shown a significant decrease in the amount of herbage consumed if harvesting is carried out less frequently. Decreases in the amounts of dry matter consumed compared with immediate feeding varied between 6-7%, 19-20% and 25-26% depending on whether the grass was cut at 24, 48 or 72 hours before feeding, respectively. This author does not however specify the type of presentation nor the method of storage of the grass (in a trailer or in heaps of different sizes).

In numerous measurements of the amounts of grass consumed indoors carried out at this Institute, (1500 measurements per week on sheep and 300 on cattle) grass was cut every morning except at weekends, and during these days a lower intake was never noted. However, the grass for sheep cut on Friday and fed on Saturday and Sunday was stored after chopping, in a coldroom at +4°C, and the grass cut for cattle on Saturday and fed long on Sunday was stored under cover in a thin layer (20 cm). It is important that the herbage does not heat during storage and that the dry matter content does not increase, as the wilting of a herbage with a low dry matter content tends to increase the amount consumed (Demarquilly, 1966; Grassland Research Institute, 1966). The recommended cutting frequency by most authors varies from once to twice daily (Meijs, 1979).

The reason for the recommendation of two cuts a day is to feed the herbage as fresh as possible and to avoid the heating which takes place during storage and in the trough. This is particularly noticeable if it is left in a heap and particularly when it has been lacerated. When herbage is cut once a day and even more so when it is cut for feeding over a period of two days (eg Saturday and Sunday), it is important to use a cold store, or to store it under cover in a thin layer, particularly in hot and humid conditions.

5.2.1.5 *Long-term storage.* Daily cutting and feeding of herbage can under certain circumstances present some difficulties which make it necessary for a whole field to be harvested and stored, for example:
— in wet areas where it is not possible to use harvesting machinery every day
— in comparing intakes of plants before and after conservation, which necessitates cutting on the same day
— in measuring the intake of forages harvested at different times of the year which have to be made simultaneously to eliminate the seasonal effects on the voluntary intake of the animal
— when rapid changes in vegetative stages of some herbages take place during intake measurements.

Only methods of storage which do not, or only slightly affect intake and nutritive value of grass can be used, namely drying and freezing.

Minson (1966) and Minson *et al* (1976) in Australia, showed that drying at 100°C for 6 hours followed by cooling for 8 hours did not affect the voluntary intake of tropical grasses by comparison with green forage. Temperatures above 100°C which can lead to a darkening of the material are not advisable. Simple driers adapted to the requirements of measuring feeding value (digestibility and intake) of fodder crops have been successfully devised in Australia. These enable drying of 0.5 tonnes of forage daily. To avoid losses and to facilitate sampling, the dried grass is coarsely chopped (2-5 cm) and blown into bags containing 4 kg of dry forage which facilitate subsequent feeding.

Demarquilly (1970) did not observe differences in digestibility or intake between fresh grass and grass artifically dehydrated at low temperature, when fed in the chopped form to sheep, but for red clover he observed a decrease of 10% in the amount consumed and 6 percentage units in digestibility. Using the same type of machine, Verite and Journet (1970) found with dairy cows, that drying led to a limited but significant increase in the amounts of dry matter consumed by comparison with fresh grass (13.62 against 13.07 kg), but this increase varied from day to day (-1.72 to $+3.82$ kg with an average of $+0.55$ kg). The difference appeared to be partly due to the presence of external moisture on the fresh plant since the increase in intake due to drying was 0.86 kg for wet grass (n = 18), and only 0.36 kg (n = 24) for grass with no surface moisture. The increase was also due to the dry matter content of fresh grass since drying only increased the amount consumed when fresh grass had a dry matter content of less than 18%. In only 2 out of 23 comparisons made by Heaney et al (1966) did drying significantly affect (one increase, one decrease) the amount of green grass-lucerne mixtures consumed.

Thus it can be concluded that although drying does not on average affect the intake of grass, it can however increase it slightly in the case of very wet grasses ($< 18\%$ DM), and sometimes decrease it in the case of legumes with a high water content which are difficult to dry. However, drying can lead to a decrease in the digestibility of organic matter and of protein. It is therefore advisable to dry at a temperature between 80 and 100°C up to a dry matter content of 87-88% as recommended by Minson et al (1976).

Freezing, when carried out rapidly, can also be used for storage of herbage and is unlikely to greatly affect the intake of herbage (Pigden et al, 1961). Heaney et al (1966) observed however a low intake of legumes after freezing, which they attributed to the high water content of the samples studied, which led to physical disruption of the cells during freezing.

Further studies are therefore necessary to establish under which conditions freezing can affect (increase or decrease) intake of green forage. The results so far however tend to confirm those of Raymond et al (1953) and Van Es and Vander Honing (1976) with grasses, that freezing does not, or only slightly modifies the digestibility of organic matter and nitrogen of herbage. However, MacRae *et al* (1975) observed in nitrogen balance trials that freezing led to an important decrease in nitrogen solubility.

5.2.2 Feeding methods

When it is necessary to know the voluntary intake of herbage it is important to make sure that the animal can effectively consume the maximum amount of herbage. Also it is important to make the most effective use of the facilities. In planning a trial the following should therefore be given consideration:
— how much herbage to offer?
— how many feeds per day and what duration of access to the feed?
— how long should preliminary and experimental periods be?
— how many animals are needed?

5.2.2.1 *Amount of herbage offered.* The term 'voluntary intake' assumes that the intake of the animal is not limited by the amount offered. It is thus necessary that the amount of herbage offered should be greater than the amount the animal is able to consume.

Tayler and Rudman (1965) showed with growing cattle kept indoors that their intake increased with the quantity offered until refusals of 25-30% occurred. Although it would seem advisable to aim for this level of refusal to ensure that the amounts consumed are near maximum, large refusals enable the animal to eat with greater selectivity. The composition and characteristics of the herbage eaten may therefore be different from that offered. This problem, which applies particularly to pastures with mixed species, is of lesser importance with young grass but becomes more relevant as the grass matures (Greenhalgh and Runcie, 1962). A reasonable compromise is achieved by feeding herbage in such amounts that refusals are not higher than 10-15% of the offered quantities (Cammell, 1977). In our studies we have opted for a 10% refusal level, but all the green forages are chopped beforehand to reduce the possibilities of selection by the animal.

5.2.2.2 *Number of feeds and time of access to feed.* As shown above, fresh herbage can satisfactorily be harvested once a day and sometimes only every two days, in order to reduce weekend work. The number of feeds offered per day is another important consideration affecting the workload. Campbell and Merilan (1961) compared the daily amounts of dry matter consumed by dairy cows fed 2, 4 or 7 times a day with lucerne hay and concentrated feeds. The highest dry matter intake of 19.1 kg was obtained with 4 feeds per day compared with 17.7 kg for 2 feeds. Increasing the number of feeds to 7 did not further increase the level of intake. However, the time of access to feed was limited to 3 hours after each feed, thus for 2 feeds, only 6 hours feeding time was available, which is inadequate to allow maximum intake, particularly for a diet rich in concentrates (60%).

Blaxter *et al* (1961) showed that when access to feed was limited to a minimum of 18 hours, the amount consumed by sheep fed 4 times at 6 hour intervals was not significantly different from the amount consumed by sheep receiving 2 equal feeds at 12 hour intervals. Similarly, Dulphy and Demarquilly (unpublished) did not observe any decrease in intake when the number of feeds per day was reduced from 3 to 2. To measure the amount of fresh herbage consumed indoors, it is therefore feasible to use a system of 2 feeds per day, with the collection and weighing of refusals every morning, before the first feed of the day. However, care must be taken where small mangers are used. The squeezing of herbage into small mangers, particularly if the herbage was harvested by a flail mower, can lead to heating in the base of the feed, and to a reduced intake.

The amount of herbage consumed depends much more on the time of access to feed than on the number of feeds. Demarquilly and Dulphy (1977) have shown that with two feeds of fresh grass per day, the intake during the two main feeding periods (each lasting 80 minutes) which follow the two feeds represents only 45-50% and 55-65% respectively for heifers and for sheep of the total daily intake. The remainder of the intake is made up with more numerous (2 to 10 depending upon herbage quality) and shorter (20 to 35 minutes) feeds spread throughout the day.

5.2.2.3   *Preliminary and experimental periods.*

There is little experimental information available for ruminants on the number of days taken to reach maximum intake levels. It is important that these levels are reached before the measurement period commences.

Blaxter *et al* (1961) showed that sheep fed on a hay of poor quality reached their maximum level of intake after 9-12 days. The same authors point out that in some experiments it can take as long as 15 days, and that daily fluctuations of intake make the definition of the timing of maximum intake difficult.

Preliminary periods of feeding normally vary from 10-14 days. The period can be reduced to 7 days for herbage studies (Demarquilly and Weiss, 1970) when the animals are already well adapted to the grass. During this period the objective of the experimenter will be to achieve the maximum level of intake as quickly as possible, feeding to a refusal of 10-15% in spite of variations in intake from day to day.

Various methods of feeding are used:
—   sequential feeding methods which consist of feeding an amount of forage equal to 1.15 times that consumed the previous two days. The

drawback to this method is that it increases the duration of the preliminary period. In the case of sudden and sporadic drops of intake (eg 30% below the intake level of the preceeding day) the amount of feed calculated for the following day is likely to be too low. For this reason Blaxter *et al* (1961) suggest a modified sequential feeding system which consists of adjusting the amount of feed for the following day, only when refusals are below 15% of the amount offered.

—   the method used at the Grassland Research Institute, Hurley (Cammell, 1977) consists of adjusting the level of feeding for a given day to 1.15 times that of 2 days before.

The experimenter must use his/her own experience to minimise the effect of daily variations in amounts consumed by changes in the amounts offered. In our studies on sheep, we aim at an average refusal of 10% (but the forages offered are chopped, which limits the possibility of selection) with daily variations between 5 and 15%.

The length of the measurement period after establishing maximum consumption is often 10-15 days, a period which results in errors of measurement of about $\pm 2\%$ (Blaxter *et al*, 1961). However, the results may not be of great value if during these periods significant changes occur in chemical composition, stage of growth and digestibility of herbage. Therefore in our series of experiments designed to study "physiological" changes with age of plant, we have opted for periods of 6 days, with an interval of one day between periods. On the day between periods when the amount consumed is not measured, it is essential that the animals are fed *ad libitum*.

5.2.2.4   *Number of animals.* It is well established that the amount of feed consumed depends on the season, the ambient temperature, and the size, breed and physiological conditions of the animal. It is thus important to standardise these parameters if the amount consumed has to reflect accurately the typical intake characteristics of the forage. In most experiments, environmental conditions are standardised across treatments and the main source of variation remaining is the variation between individual animals.

The variations in intake between animals is important in deciding how many animals are required per treatment. For sheep the coefficient of variation for intake of conserved forages varies between 10 and 15%, excluding results for straw and silage (Crampton *et al*, 1960; Blaxter *et al*, 1961; Heaney *et al*, 1968). It seems however that the variability is slightly less for fresh forages. Michalet-Doreau and Demarquilly (unpublished) have calculated the variability of the measurements of the amounts consumed using 26 different lots of 6 sheep, each of which had received 50 samples of fresh forage chosen at random among 1200 samples studied in their laboratory. The standard deviation (SD) was 6.9 g/kg $W^{0.75}$ and the coefficient of variation (CV) 9%. This variability is smaller than that (10.5%) calculated by Minson *et al* (1964). The variation can be decreased (SD = 4.9; CV = 7%) if the values which differ from the mean by more than two standard deviations are ignored. Using this premise it was possible to draw two curves (Fig. 5.1) which give the number of animals necessary to detect a given difference in the amounts consumed. With 6 sheep per group it is possible to detect differences of 11 g/kg $W^{0.75}$ (curve 1) and of 8 g/kg $W^{0.75}$ (curve 2) in intake at the 5% significance level.

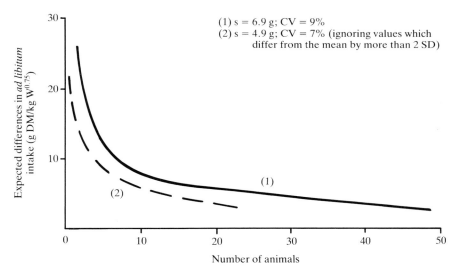

Fig. 5.1   *Number of animals required to give an 80% probability that the intake difference will be sufficient at the 5% level (Michalet-Doreau and Demarquilly, unpublished).*

Some workers (eg Minson *et al*, 1976) have used 8-10 sheep per trial, but because of the complexity involved, most authors work with 6 animals per trial. This number has been adopted by Demarquilly and Weiss (1970) to establish the French tables of feeding values for forage. This number was also recommended by Heaney (1979).

5.2.3   The value and use of measurements of herbage intake

When a measure of the amount consumed is obtained for a given forage, the value may be used for the following:
—   to describe the true intake characteristics of forage

— to extrapolate this value to other types of animals or other species

As discussed earlier, the amount of a forage voluntarily consumed by a ruminant depends not only on the intake characteristics of this forage (called "ingestibility" but also on the "ingestive capacity" (often wrongly called appetite) of the animal on which the measurement is made. This ingestive capacity depends on the following:

— weight, age, physiological state (growth, lactation, fattening) and feeding history of the animal, as well as species and breed
— environmental conditions (climate, season, indoor conditions) in which the measurements are made

The sources of variation related to environmental conditions can be easily eliminated if care is taken to make the measurements at the same period of time and under the same environmental conditions, as for example when comparing the intake of species or varieties of plants grown around the same time. However, when differences are found in the intake of herbages grown at different times of the year, these could be attributed to differences in herbage characteristics, to different animal characteristics, or to different environmental conditions. If the real reason for these differences needs to be known, the answer can only be obtained by making measurements at the same time, of the quantities consumed of corresponding dried or frozen herbage or by comparison with the intake of a standard forage (for example a standard hay).

Other sources of variation related to the animal (except for liveweight), are more difficult to eliminate. The effect of liveweight can be easily accounted for by expressing the amount consumed per kg of metabolic weight ($W^{0.75}$). This notation has been adopted by most of the authors interested in intake of feeds since it was recommended at the 3rd Symposium of Energy Metabolism (Kleiber, 1965).

Other factors can also affect the voluntary intake of the animal, namely age and physiological state, stage of lactation and level of milk production, stage of fattening and feeding history, and also breed. This implies that measurements of amounts consumed indoors should be made on:

— animals as similar as possible to those for which it is necessary to know the amount consumed
— "standard" animals, as comparable as possible from one experiment to another if the main interest is variations in herbage intake in relation to age, growth stage, number of cuts of the plant, type of herbage. In the case of long term experiments, "standard" animals will have to be changed periodically

The majority of researchers interested in the intake of forage plants have for reasons of ease and cost, measured intakes on castrated male sheep.

These intakes expressed in g/kg $W^{0.75}$ are not directly applicable to cattle and lactating ewes. However, the ranking of the intakes observed with castrated male sheep tend to remain the same for other categories of ruminants (Blaxter and Wilson, 1962; Blaxter *et al*, 1966; Buchman and Henken, 1964; Ingalls *et al*, 1965; Demarquilly and Weiss, 1971). Also intakes measured on sheep can be quantitatively related to the amounts consumed by cattle. Intake measurements made simultaneously on "standard" sheep (castrated Texel rams, 1.5-3 years old and weighing on average 60 kg) and cattle at CRZV at Theix showed a close relationship between intake of forage by cattle (y) and intake by sheep (x), the two values being expressed in g DM/kg $W^{0.75}$ (Fig. 5.2). These relationships can be expressed by the following two equations:

Dairy cows of 600 kg producing 17 kg of milk —

$$y = 57.8 + 0.851 \times (\pm 8.20; n = 66; r = 0.82) \tag{5.1}$$

Fattening cattle from 300 to 450 kg —

$$y = 31.4 + 0.919 \times (\pm 6.2; n = 71; r = 0.93) \tag{5.2}$$

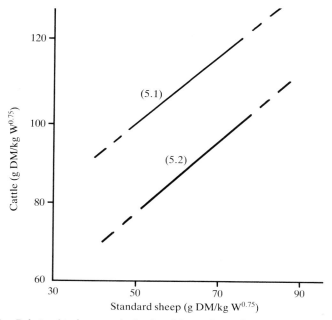

Fig. 5.2   *Relationship between the intake of forage by cattle and by standard sheep (INRA, Departement d'Elevage des Ruminants, 1979)*

These equations have been used to establish the system "des unités d'encombrement" (UE), or fill units. This enables the voluntary intake of various categories of ruminants expressed in UE, and the intake of the various forages also expressed in UE, to be estimated whether these forages are fed alone or together with concentrated feeding stuffs (INRA, Département d'Elevage des Ruminants, 1979).

5.3 THE USE OF MEASUREMENTS OF HERBAGE INTAKE MADE INDOORS TO ESTIMATE INTAKE BY THE GRAZING ANIMAL

The measurement of intake of a fresh herbage made indoors can be a useful guide to the total amount which can be voluntarily consumed by the animal. It can also be used for the comparison and classification of different herbages. However, the relationship between the intake of herbage fed indoors and the intake of the same herbage grazed *in situ* is much more complex as the amount consumed during grazing will be affected by a range of additional factors, and in particular by the grazing pressure (the number of animals in relation to the amount of herbage available).

The relationship between quantity of grass available and quantity of grass consumed by ruminants at pasture can be considered as asymptotic (Hodgson, 1976). Curves (Fig. 5.3) drawn for growing cattle (Marsh and Murdoch, 1974) show that the relationships between amounts consumed and amount offered is curvilinear up to values for amounts offered of 5-6 kg DM/100 kg liveweight. It is therefore not possible to use a measure of the amount of herbage consumed indoors to give an estimate of the amount consumed by the grazing animal.

The feeding conditions of the grazing animal are very different from those of the indoor animal, mainly because more herbage selection occurs during grazing, although this varies according to grazing pressure. The lower the stocking rate the greater the opportunity for the animal to be selective, ie to choose the most digestible or palatable plants or parts of plants, which results in a greater consumption of nutrients. Also at a given grazing pressure, selectivity will depend on the following:

— stage of growth of herbage: selection will be less if the grass is young and leafy (Greenhalgh and Runcie, 1962) because the morphological composition of the plant is more uniform. Differences in digestibility of the various parts of the plant are smaller at the leafy stage (Demarquilly and Chenost, 1969; Chenost *et al*, 1970), than later when lignification of the stems is rapid (Jarrige and Minson, 1964)

— type of pasture: selection will be limited in the case of a homogeneous canopy, possibilities of selection being smaller in pure swards than in mixed swards

— animal species: sheep have a greater ability to select than cattle; this ability is particularly important in the case of a less dense and less green canopy (Dudzinski and Arnold, 1973).

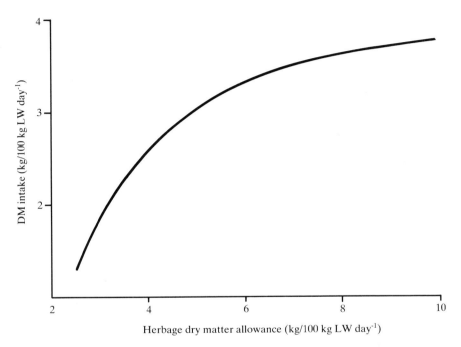

Fig. 5.3   Relationship between dry matter intake by steers at pasture and herbage dry matter allowance (Marsh and Murdoch, 1974).

However, when conditions of pasture utilization are such that grazing pressure is relatively high but intake is not restricted (percentage of refusals higher than that allowed indoors, but within the same order of magnitude), the intake in grazing conditions seems to be similar to that observed indoors.

This is shown by the results of Greenhalgh and Runcie (1962) and by Greenhalgh *et al*(1972) (Table 5.6). The herbage intake by dairy cows and growing cattle either at pasture (strip or rotational grazing) or zero grazed were of the same magnitude, where herbage allowance and stocking rates were similar in the two cases.

These results are confirmed by those of Demarquilly (1963; 1966) who observed that milk production and milk composition for housed cows fed on grass showed the same variation as grazing cows fed on the same grass, but milk production was lower for cows fed indoors than for grazing cows. Measurement of the amount of grass consumed indoors is thus likely to be an underestimate of that consumed at pasture.

Table 5.6 *Quantities of herbage consumed (kg OM day^{-1}) by dairy cows and growing cattle either strip grazed or zero-grazed, at similar stocking rates and herbage allowances*

(a) dairy cows — mixed sward of cocksfoot, perennial ryegrass, white and red clover (Greenhalgh and Runcie, 1962)

Cut no	Strip grazing (allowance for maximum intake)	Zero grazing (refusal of about 20%)
1	12.2	12.5
2	12.4	11.6
3	13.3	13.5
4	12.9	12.1
5	13.2	12.3
Mean	12.8	12.4

(b) growing cattle — pure perennial ryegrass (Greenhalgh *et al*, 1972)

Cut no	Rotational grazing (C)*	(V)*	Zero grazing (Z)*
1	7.03	7.39	6.42
2	5.50	6.59	7.20
3	6.50	6.87	6.13
4	5.15	6.30	6.18
Mean	6.18	6.87	6.54

* (C) (Z) = same stocking rate
  (V)   = stocking rate continuously varied to give the same liveweight gain per animal as group Z.

It is possible to use values of the amounts consumed indoors to estimate the relative amounts consumed by grazing animals. It is also possible to examine by this method variations which occur for grass species, botanical composition, stage of utilization, age of herbage, number of cuts, season etc. The amount consumed indoors on occasions may be higher than that consumed at grazing in the case of plants whose palatability at pasture can be limited by the presence of awns, spines, and by growth habit and plant texture. For example, tall fescue is consumed more easily when chopped and fed indoors than when grazed.

Finally, measurements made indoors have little or no value when the grazing animal can be selective, which is the case when it grazes range, natural pastures, savannahs etc.

5.4 REFERENCES

BLAXTER, K L, WAINMAN, F W and WILSON, R S (1961). The regulation of food intake by sheep. *Animal Production*, 3, 51-61.

BLAXTER, K L and WILSON, R S (1962). The voluntary intake of roughages by steers. *Animal Production*, 4, 351-358.

BLAXTER, K L, WAINMAN, F W and DAVIDSON, J L (1966). The voluntary intake of food by sheep and cattle in relation to their energy requirements for maintenance. *Animal Production*, 8, 75-83.

BUCHMAN, D T and HEMKEN, R W (1964). *Ad libitum* intake and digestibility of several alfalfa hays by cattle and sheep. *Journal of Dairy Science*, 47, 861-864.

CAMMELL, S B (1977). Equipment and techniques used for research into the intake and digestion of forages by sheep and calves. *Technical Report No 24, Grassland Research Institute, Hurley, Maidenhead*.

CAMPBELL, J R and MERILAN, C P (1961). Effect of frequency of feeding on production characteristics and feed utilization in lactating dairy cows. *Journal of Dairy Science*, 44, 664-671.

CHENOST, M and DEMARQUILLY, C (1969). Comparison entre le pâturage et l'affouragement en vert pour la production de viande bovine. *Annales de Zootechnie*, 18, 277-298.

CHENOST, M, GRENET, Elisabeth, DEMARQUILLY, C and JARRIGE, R (1970). The use of nylon bag technique for the study of forage digestion in the rumen and for predicting feed value. *Proceedings of the 11th International Grassland Congress*, 697-701.

COLLINS, D P (1973). Zerograzing of beef cattle. *An Foras Taluntais*, 35-36.

CRAMPTON, E W, DONEFER, F and LLOYD, L E (1960). A nutritive value index for forages. *Journal of Animal Science*, 19, 538-544.

DEMARQUILLY, C (1963). Influence de la nature du pâturage sur la production laitière et la composition du lait. *Annales de Zootechnie*, 12, 69-104.

DEMARQUILLY, C (1966). Valeur alimentaire de l'herbe des prairies temporaires aux stades d'exploitation pour le pâturage. II — Quantité ingérée par les vaches laitières. *Annales de Zootechnie*, 15, 147-169.

DEMARQUILLY, C (1970). Influence de la déshydratation à basse temperature sur la valeur alimentaire des fourrages. *Annales de Zootechnie*, 19, 45-51.

DEMARQUILLY, C and CHENOST, M (1969). Étude de la digestion de fourrages dans le rumen par le méthode des sachets de nylon. Liaisons avec la valeur alimentaire. *Annales de Zootechnie*, 18, 419-436.

DEMARQUILLY, C and DULPHY, J P (1977). Effect of ensiling on feed intake and animal performances. *Proceedings of the 1st International Meeting on Animal Production from Temperate Grassland, Dublin*, pp 53-61.

DEMARQUILLY, C and WEISS, Ph (1970). Tableaux de la valeur alimentaire des fourrages. *Ministere de l'Agriculture, I.N.R.A., SEI, étude n° 42, M3 Fourr. 53, Po Elev. 311*.

DEMARQUILLY, C and WEISS, Ph (1971). Liaisons entre les quantités de matière sèche de fourrages verts ingérées par les moutons et celles ingérées par les bovins. *Annales de Zootechnie*, 20, 119-134.

DUDZINSKI, M L and ARNOLD, G W (1973). Comparison of diets of sheep and cattle grazing together on sown pastures on the southern tablelands of New South Wales by principal components analysis. *Australian Journal of Agricultural Research*, 24, 899-912.

GRASSLANDS RESEARCH INSTITUTE (1966). *Annual Report of the Grassland Research Institute, Hurley, Maidenhead 1966* pp 41-42.

GREENHALGH, J F D and RUNCIE, K V (1962). The herbage intake and milk production of strip and zerograzed dairy cows. *Journal of Agricultural Science, Cambridge*, 59, 95-103.

GREENHALGH, J F D, AITKEN, J N and REID, G W (1972). A note on the zero-grazing of beef cattle. *Journal of the British Grassland Society*, 27, 173-177.

HEANEY, D P (1979). Sheep as pilot animals. *Proceedings of the Workshop on standardization of analytical methodology for feeds*, pp 45-48, Ottawa 12-14 March 1979, Ed W J Pigden, C C Balch and Michael Graham, IDRC — 134e.

HEANEY, D P, PIGDEN, W J and PRITCHARD, G I (1966). The effect of freezing or drying pasture herbage on digestibility and voluntary intake assays with sheep. *Proceedings of the 10th International Grassland Congress, Helsinki, Section 2, Paper 7*.

HEANEY, D P, PRITCHARD, G I and PIGDEN, W J (1968). Variability in *ad libitum* forages intake by sheep. *Journal of Animal Science*, 27, 159-164.

HODGSON, J (1976). *In Pasture utilization by the grazing animal* (ed J Hodgson and D K Jackson), pp 93 British Grassland Society Occasional Symposium, No 8.

HUTTON, J B (1962). Studies on the nutritive value of New Zealand dairy pastures. II. Herbage intake and digestibility studies with dry cattle. *New Zealand Journal of Agricultural Research*, 5, 409-424.

INGALLS, J R, THOMAS, J W and TESAR, M B (1965). Comparison of responses to various forages by sheep, rabbits and heifers. *Journal of Animal Science*, 24, 1165-1168.

INRA, Department d'Elevage des Ruminants (1979). Le système des unités d'encombrement pour les bovins. *Bull Techn CRZV Theix, INRA*, 38, 57-79.

JARRIGE, R and MINSON, D J (1964). Digestibilité des constituants du ray-grass anglais 24 et du dactyle S37, plus spécialement des constituants glucidiques. *Annales de Zootechnie*, 13, 117-150.

KLEIBER, M (1965). Metabolic body size. *In 3rd Symposium of Energy Metabolism*, pp 427-435. Ed K L Blaxter, London, New York, Academic Press.

MacRAE, J C, CAMPBELL, D R and EADIE, J (1975). Changes in the biochemical composition of herbage upon freezing and thawing. *Journal of Agricultural Science, Cambridge*, 84, 125-131.

MARSH, R and MURDOCH, J C (1974). Effect of high fertilizer nitrogen and stocking rate on liveweight gain per animal and per hectare. *Journal of the British Grassland Society*, 29, 305-313.

MEIJS, J A C (1979). Advances in the direct techniques to estimate herbage intake. *European Grazing Workshop, 2-5 April 1979, Lelystad*.

MINSON, D J (1966). The intake and nutritive value of fresh, frozen and dried *Sorghum almum, Digitaria decumbens,* and *Panicum maximum. Journal of the British Grassland Society*, 21, 123-126.

MINSON, D J, HARRIS, C E, RAYMOND, W R and MILFORD, R (1964). The digestibility and voluntary intake of S 22 and H 1 ryegrass, S 170 tall fescue, S 48 timothy, S 215 meadow fescue and germinal cocksfoot. *Journal of the British Grassland Society*, 19, 298-305.

MINSON, D J, STOBBS, T H, HEGARTY, M P and PLAYNE, M J (1976). Measuring the nutritive value of pasture plants. *Tropical Pasture Research, Principles and Methods, Bulletin 51, Chapter 13, Commonwealth Agricultural Bureaux*.

PIGDEN, W J, PRITCHARD, G I, WINTER, K A and LOGAN, U S (1961). Freezing — a technique for forage investigations. *Journal of Animal Science*, 4, 796-801.

RAYMOND, W F, HARRIS, C E and HARKER, V G (1953). Studies on the digestibility of herbage. II. Effect of freezing and cold storage of herbage on its digestibility by sheep. *Journal of the British Grassland Society*, 8, 315-320.

TAYLER, J C and RUDMAN, J E (1965). Height and method of cutting or grazing in relation to herbage consumption and liveweight gain. *Proceedings of the 9th International Grassland Congress, Sao Paulo*, 20 pp 1639-1644.

VAN ES, A J H, and VAN DER HONING, Y (1976). Energy and nitrogen balances of lactating cows fed fresh or frozen grass in *Energy Metabolism of Farm Animals*, pp 838. *Proceedings of the 7th Symposium EAAP, Vichy, France, September 1976*.

VERITE, R and JOURNET, M (1970). Influence de la teneur en eau et de la déshydratation de l'herbe sur sa valeur alimentaire pour les vaches laitières. *Annales de Zootechnie*, 19, 255-268.

ZEMMELINK, G (1980). Effect of selective consumption on voluntary intake and digestibility of tropical forages. *Agricultural Research Report 896, Centre for Agricultural Publishing and Documentation, Pudoc, Wageningen*.

CHAPTER 6

INGESTIVE BEHAVIOUR

J. Hodgson

6.1 INTRODUCTION

The daily consumption of herbage by a grazing animal (I) can be viewed as the product of three variables: the time spent grazing (GT), the rate of biting during grazing (RB) and herbage intake per bite (IB), thus:

$$I = GT \times RB \times IB \tag{6.1}$$

Two additional variables can be calculated from the components of equation 6.1. They are a) the total number of grazing bites per day (B), the product of GT and RB, and b) the rate of herbage intake (RI), the product of RB and IB. These five variables, which collectively describe ingestive behaviour, are considered in this chapter. Other aspects of the behaviour of grazing animals, some of which may be closely related to the feeding process (eg locomotion and rumination), are not considered. For wider coverage of the subject the reader is referred to comprehensive reviews by Hancock (1953), Hafez (1969) and Arnold and Dudzinski (1978).

The above view of ingestive behaviour (Spedding *et al,* 1966; Allden and Whittaker, 1970) is somewhat mechanistic. However, it reduces the complex behaviour patterns of the grazing process to a simple series of quantifiable functions, and thus provides a useful basis for considering the way in which behavioural responses to variations in sward characteristics may influence herbage intake. In the absence of error the product (GT x RB x IB) in equation 6.1 should equate to I, and in theory it should be possible to calculate any single variable in the equation from a knowledge of the other three. Chacon *et al* (1976) have shown that it is technically possible to estimate herbage intake from information on the components of ingestive behaviour (Chapter 3), and IB has been estimated from information on I and B (Jamieson and Hodgson, 1979b). However, the error-free state is not easy to achieve, and it is probably prudent to think of measurements of ingestive behaviour as a means of explaining observed effects on herbage intake rather than as a means of estimating intake itself, and to measure intake independently by any of the methods outlined elsewhere in this book.

The choice of procedures for recording grazing behaviour is strongly influenced by considerations of convenience, flexibility, comprehensiveness and cost. Many techniques have been developed over the years to measure one or more of the components of equation 6.1, and the rapid developments in electronic recording systems have greatly improved the opportunities for making detailed observations on aspects of ingestive behaviour. Practical aspects of the alternative techniques are discussed later in this chapter. However, the characteristics of the grazing process dictate a number of principles which are common to all procedures, and which must be taken into account in determining how any particular technique is applied in the field. These principles are considered first.

6.2 GRAZING ACTIVITY

The working day of a grazing animal is divided into alternating periods of grazing, ruminating and rest, and the duration and to some extent the distribution of grazing and ruminating activity may be influenced by sward conditions, grazing management and climatic variation. Patterns of activity typical of many observed on temperate swards are shown in Figure 6.1. The activity patterns of the individual members of a group are usually similar, and the timing of the main periods of grazing is strongly influenced by the time of sunrise and sunset (Hafez, 1969; Arnold, 1981). The intensity of activity may vary within and between each of the main grazing periods (see section 6.3.3), and recording procedures should be designed with this variation in mind.

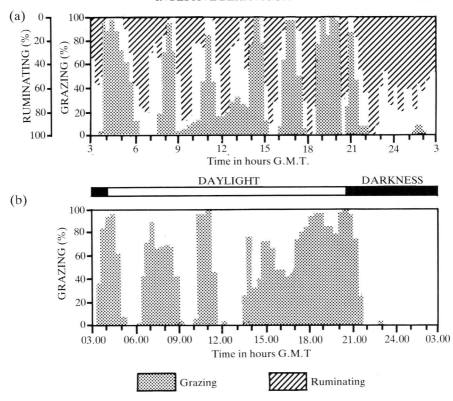

Fig. 6.1   Diurnal patterns of grazing activity in (a) cattle and (b) sheep (from Hafez, 1968)

Grazing is itself a complex activity in which the relative amount and distribution of time spent actually taking mouthfuls of herbage, and that spent in the associated activities of searching for suitable herbage and manipulating it in the mouth, can be very variable. External stimuli like weather conditions and the presence of other animals may interfere with ingestive behaviour to a variable and unpredictable degree. Jaw activity during grazing is also complex, since it involves movements to arrange herbage in the mouth for biting, and movements to masticate severed herbage and arrange it for swallowing, in addition to the straightforward action involved in gripping herbage between the lower incisors and the dental pad in preparation for the jerk of the head which severs it from the sward.

    All of these items properly contribute to characteristic grazing behaviour, but they can make for considerable difficulties when attempting to measure and describe the components of ingestive behaviour. Most of the difficulties relate to the need to define biting activity objectively, and hence the rate of biting and the duration of a period of grazing. This may seem to be a rather esoteric point, and indeed there is no general agreement at present about the definitions to be adopted. However, the need to use as strict a definition as possible of the variable(s) under study, and to write this down for reference, cannot be over-emphasised. As will be seen, the problem of definition is common to all methods of monitoring ingestive behaviour; it is as great in automatic procedures, which may be considered to be objective, as in manual procedures which frequently are not.

Observations on the number or frequency of biting movements are dependent upon an adequate definition of a "bite" which makes sense in biological terms, and which is also amenable to recording. Attention may be concentrated on movement of the jaw (eg Stobbs and Cowper, 1972) or the head (eg Chambers *et al*, 1981), or some combination of the two. Head movements are easier to see than jaw movements, but may not be so easy to record automatically. The relative numbers and distribution of biting and manipulative jaw movements appear to differ in sheep and cattle and to vary with changing sward conditions (Chacon *et al*, 1976; Chambers *et al* 1981; Table 6.1). Chacon *et al* (1976) divided manipulative movements into those made with the head down and those with the head up (6-11% and 17-22% of total grazing jaw movements respectively). The definition of a bite as head movement associated with the severence of a bunch of herbage (or an individual leaf) gripped in the mouth has the merit of objectivity, but may not always be the most appropriate, and many automatic recording devices make use of jaw movement rather than head movement (section 6.6).

Table 6.1 The ratio of jaw (biting plus manipulating) movements to head (biting) movements during grazing in sheep and cattle grazing on several swards. (from Chambers et al, 1981).

Sheep					
Sward height (cm)	4	6	12		
Ratio jaw : head movements	1.7	1.7	3.0		
± S E	0.08	0.12	0.17		
Cattle					
Trial		(a)		(b)	
Sward height (cm)	9	13	15	9	19
Ratio jaw : head movements	1.2	1.1	1.7	1.5	1.2
± S E	0.05	0.03	0.18	0.07	0.08

Biting during bouts of grazing is frequently intermittent. An animal may interrupt its biting activity to move to a new area of vegetation, to move out of the way of another animal, or in response to any one of a number of disturbance factors. Interruptions of this kind tend to be more frequent and of longer duration at the beginning and end of a grazing period than in the middle. Thus the identification of the commencement and cessation of grazing (and hence of grazing time) and the assessment of rate of biting during grazing are dependent upon the maximum interval between bites which is considered to be acceptable as a part of normal grazing activity.

No single definition of biting activity is of general application, but for any given circumstances it is desirable to arrive at as objective a definition as possible and to apply it consistently. In practice it is usually advisable to concentrate attention on the active ingestion of herbage, excluding as far as possible any intervals over which the active grazing process is interrupted. The extreme case would be to exclude the time for which an animal simply raises its head to manipulate a mouthful of grass before swallowing it. However, in many cases it would be unrealistic to exclude the time for which an animal is actively but unsuccessfully seeking acceptable mouthfuls of herbage to bite and it would then be appropriate to record grazing activity whenever an animal is biting herbage, or moving with its muzzle close to the sward. For observations on grazing time or periodicity it may often be convenient to include the intervals when an animal is masticating herbage with its head raised preparatory to continuing to graze more herbage, so long as the maximum interval is defined. It is important to use the **same** definition for estimates of grazing time, number of bites and biting rate within a study or, where there are good reasons for adopting different standards, to ensure that the differences are fully explained. The maximum acceptable interval between bites may be determined by the recording system used; it will depend upon whether head or jaw movements are monitored, for instance. The use to be made of the records will also affect the decision.

6.2.1 Grazing time (GT)

Estimates of the time spent grazing may be derived from the continuous monitoring of activity or by using an interval sampling technique. The former is likely to be the more accurate, but is difficult to carry out unless automatic equipment is available. In interval recording it is assumed that each record is representative of activity over the time interval since the previous record, and recording intervals must be set to limit the risk of substantial end-point errors. Gary *et al* (1970) found no significant differences between estimates of grazing time derived from observation at intervals of 1, 15, 30 and 45 min, and concluded that observation at 15 min intervals provide a reliable measure of "characters of a continuous nature" like grazing. However, recording intervals of 5-10 min are commonly preferred, particularly where the periodicity of grazing activity is of interest. A comparison of estimates of grazing time from continuous observation and observation at 5 min and 10 min intervals is given in Table 6.2.

Table 6.2 Recording interval and the determination of grazing time (from Jamieson, 1975).

Recording procedure	Grazing time (h)[+]
Continuous	7.50
5 min interval	7.47
10 min interval	7.42
S.E.	0.130

[+]Between 0500 h and 2100 h; means of 5 cows x 5 recording days.

Continuous records indicate the start and finish of each period of grazing, given an objective definition of grazing activity. In an intermittent recording system it will often be necessary to observe an animal or monitor a record for some seconds before it is possible to determine the current activity pattern with certainty, and this is likely to be of greatest importance close to times of transition from one activity to another. Thus any intermittent system, manual or automatic, should allow for a "dwell time" on each individual. However, it is important not to wait too long for an animal to "make up its mind". It is difficult to set a maximum dwell time, and with experience, the periods of irresolution become relatively few; a period of 5-10 sec seems reasonable.

6.2.2 Rate of biting (RB)

The mean rate of biting over 24 h or a full grazing period may be calculated from the total grazing time and the total number of bites taken, though the latter can only realistically be measured using an automatic recording technique. Normally, however, rate of biting would be estimated over short periods of time, often at intervals during the day (section 6.3.3) and the need then is to determine the criteria under which measurements will be made.

The difficulty of arriving at a definition of biting activity which allows an objective measurement of biting rate was discussed earlier. One approach is to record the total number of bites which occur in a fixed time interval, but a measure of this kind is not always easy to relate to estimates of grazing time. In manual recording systems it is easier to record the time taken to complete a specified number of bites, and it is then necessary to specify the maximum interval between bites which will be accepted for the record to continue. It is not easy to give general guidance on this question, but the point can be illustrated by quoting the results of two techniques described by Jamieson and Hodgson (1979a) for grazing calves. Estimates of biting rate derived from records of the time taken to make 20 uninterrupted bites were on average 16% greater than estimates derived from the total number of bites made in a 2 min period, with the proviso that a record was discarded if an animal failed to bite for more than 1 min (53.4 vs 45.9 $\pm$ 0.59 bites min^{-1}). The former record was taken as an indication of the maximal biting rate for the sward in question. These examples illustrate two relatively objective alternative definitions, but others are possible to suit particular circumstances.

The shorter the period of counting the greater the end-point errors of an estimate of biting rate, but the greater will be the risks of a genuine change in the pattern of activity. Also, in manual procedures counting periods of longer than 2-3 min make heavy demands on the concentration and mobility of observers. The period chosen will depend upon circumstances; in most situations a range from 0.5 to 3 min (or 20-150 bites) seems reasonable, but shorter sequences of bites have been used successfully (section 6.4.2).

6.2.3 Total grazing bites (B)

The total number of grazing bites over 24 h or some shorter interval of time may be measured directly, or calculated as the product of grazing time (GT) and the mean rate of biting (RB) over time. The former approach is only realistic for automatic recording procedures. The latter may be used for both manual and automatic techniques, but in this case it is important to ensure that the criteria for determining grazing activity and estimating bite rate are compatible.

6.2.4 Rate of intake (RI) and intake per bite (IB)

The rate of herbage intake (weight per unit time) may be calculated as a daily average value from estimates of daily herbage intake (I) divided by daily grazing time (GT), or measured directly over short periods of time. Estimates of intake per bite are obtained by dividing intake by the number of grazing bites recorded over the appropriate time interval. The procedures for measuring grazing time and biting rate or total bites have been discussed in general terms. The additional procedures necessary for the estimation of rate of intake and intake per bite are outlined here.

6.2.4.1 *Calculation from estimates of daily herbage intake, grazing time and total bites.* Estimates of rate of intake and intake per bite made using these procedures are susceptible to the cumulative errors of estimation of the variables used in the calculations (see chapter 3 and this chapter). Calculation of rate of intake and intake per bite in this way involves least direct interference with experimental animals, and is convenient when the basic intake and behaviour information is already available. This procedure may provide less biased estimates of the long-run mean values. There is a risk that calculation of the product of rate of biting and grazing time will overestimate total daily bites, resulting in an under estimate of intake per bite (Jamieson and Hodgson, 1979a), though this is not always the case (Table 6.3).

Table 6.3 Intake per bite of grazing calves (mg OM kg LW^{-1}) estimated by two different methods (from Jamieson and Hodgson, 1979b).

Sward	I		II			III		S.E.
Week	1	2	3	4	5	6	7	week mean
Intake per bite (mg OM kg LW^{-1}) estimated on:								
Fistulates[+]	1.66	1.34	0.78	0.67	0.88	0.47	0.76	0.074
Non-fistulates[ø]	1.26	1.07	0.84	0.72	0.63	0.63	0.74	0.074

+By extrusa collection;
øBy calculation from daily herbage intake and daily bites; for details see text.

6.2.4.2 *Short-term estimates.* Short-term estimates of rate of intake or intake per bite may be made using animals harnessed to prevent the loss of faeces and urine (Allden and Whittaker, 1970), or by the collection of swallowed herbage at a fistula in the oesophagus (Stobbs, 1973), in both cases in association with the appropriate measurements of grazing time and bite number. Further details are given in section 6.4.3.

Both of these procedures tend to condition the animals to graze and, indeed, they are dependent upon the rapid resumption of grazing activity when animals are placed on sampling areas. Since biting rate and rate of intake may both be relatively high at the beginning of a grazing period (section 6.3.3) it seems likely that both procedures will tend to over-estimate true daily mean values for the two parameters (Table 6.3). These short-term estimates are independent of other animal measurements and can be directly related to sward measurements made at the same time. In addition, appropriate allocation procedures using change-over designs make it possible to estimate treatment and animal effects independently and should thus improve the precision of the estimates.

6.3 EXPERIMENTAL VARIATION

An indication of the range of values to be expected for the components of ingestive behaviour in cattle and sheep grazing temperate swards is given in Table 6.4. The range for individual records will be greater than this. Table 6.5 indicates the magnitude of the residual variation (expressed as the coefficient of variation (CV) for each component. For further information see Arnold (1981).

Table 6.4 Examples of ranges of values of ingestive behaviour variables measured on cattle and sheep grazing temperate swards (from Jamieson, 1975).

Variable	Sheep[+]	Cattle[ø]
Grazing time (h d^{-1})	9.1 – 12.3	5.8 – 10.1
Biting rate (bites min^{-1})	31 – 49	21 – 66
Total daily bites (10^3)[§]	17 – 34	8 – 36
Intake per bite[†]		
(mg OM)	11 – 400	70 – 1610
(mg OM kg LW^{-1})	0.6 – 1.5	0.3 – 4.1
Rate of intake[†]		
(mg OM kg LW^{-1} min^{-1})	33 – 54	13 – 204

[+]Weaned lambs
[ø]Weaned calves and lactating cows
[§]Biting rate x grazing time
[†]Cattle: extrusa collections from fistulated animals
 Sheep: by calculation from daily intake and total daily bites.

Table 6.5 Examples of the ranges of within-treatment variability, expressed as the coefficient of variation (CV %) of ingestive behaviour variables measured on cattle and sheep grazing temperate swards (from Jamieson, 1975).

Variable	Sheep	Cattle
Grazing time	5 – 7	5 – 7
Biting rate	8 – 11	4 – 12
Total daily bites	8 – 12	6 – 12
Intake per bite	16 – 32	7 – 30
Rate of intake	—	7 – 18

Intake per bite shows the greatest variation across treatments, and also the greatest residual variation. This parameter usually exerts a dominant influence upon daily herbage intake, and in most circumstances compensating changes in biting rate and grazing time are inadequate to offset changes in intake per bite (Fig. 6.2).

When the effects of sward or management differences are removed, all of the components of ingestive behaviour can vary between individual animals, between days and, in the case of short-term variables like biting rate, within and between grazing periods during the day. In order to make comparisons between experimental treatments as accurately as possible it is important that these additional sources of variation should be eliminated or, alternatively, identified and isolated. Ways of doing this are discussed briefly here. The CV's shown in Table 6.5 are the residuals after allowing as far as possible for consistent animal, day and period effects.

Ingestive behaviour
and Herbage intake

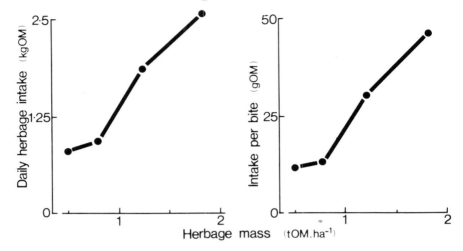

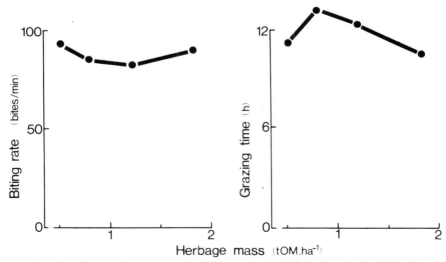

Fig. 6.2 The influence of variations in herbage mass on (a) daily herbage intake, (b) intake per bite, (c) rate of biting and (d) grazing time in ewes grazing continuously stocked swards (from Bircham, 1981)

6.3.1 **Individual animal variation**

It is helpful to estimate the magnitude of consistent differences between individual animals within a group whenever possible, and the simplest way of doing so is to make repeated measurements on the same animals over a series of days or periods within a day. In order to isolate animal and treatment effects it is necessary to use a change-over design (see Snedecor and Cochran, 1967), but this is not always easy to do (cf Combellas and Hodgson, 1979; Le Du *et al*, 1979).

Where between-animal differences can be determined, observations on 4-6 animals per treatment would normally be adequate to define between-treatment differences for most behaviour parameters with an acceptable degree of precision. With these numbers, and particularly with variables like intake per bite which have an inherently large variation (Tables 6.4 & 6.5), it is advisable to make repeat measurements within treatment periods. For less efficient designs (ie where cross-overs are not possible) larger numbers of animals will be required; more observations per animal will be of limited value.

6.3.2 **Between-day variation**

Between-day variation may reflect minor differences in management, which might have been avoided, and in weather conditions, which cannot (Gary *et al*, 1970). It is always advisable to make repeat measurements over two or more days in a measurement period in order to reduce the risks of biased estimates of particular behaviour variables resulting from peculiar weather conditions. Conventional measurements of herbage intake are normally made over periods of 7-14 days, and where related measurements of behaviour are to be made it is sensible to spread them out over a comparable time period.

6.3.3 **Within-day variation**

The rate of biting may be faster in the morning and evening than for the rest of the day (Rodriquez Capriles, 1973), and may tend to decline with time during a grazing period (Hancock, 1950). These patterns are not always observed (Jamieson, 1975), but it is important to take them into account in planning operational schedules in order to ensure adequate balance in the data. Records should cover at least the major grazing periods of the day, including particularly those in the early morning and in the evening and, if possible, repeated observations should be made on individual animals at intervals during any one grazing period.

6.4 OBSERVATION OF GRAZING ACTIVITY

Most individuals with an interest in animal behaviour start by watching animals, and indeed a detailed knowledge of behaviour patterns derived from direct observation is an essential prerequisite to the collection and analysis of grazing records, by whatever means. Direct observation is laborious and frequently uncomfortable, and tends to be abandoned in favour of automatic procedures as quickly as possible. Its major limitations are (a) restrictions to the duration of periods of observation because of labour demands, and (b) the difficulty of maintaining concentration for long periods of time, and hence the need for teams of observers with a consequent risk of individual variation in the interpretation of grazing activity. However, it has the merits of extreme flexibility and adaptability, and is not to be dismissed lightly.

Generally speaking, definition of grazing activity is relatively easy up to distances of 50-100 m with the naked eye, and 200-250 m with binoculars, so long as a clear field of view is maintained. Observations on biting rates may require closer approach. Binoculars with 7 x 50 magnification are best suited to the purpose. They should be light, and zoom focus is an advantage. Higher magnification increases the problem of image shake which can only be overcome by the use of a tripod, and this limits mobility. In order to ensure a good field of view at all times it is often necessary for the observer to be mobile, and equipment and observation points should be planned with this in mind. However, there is evidence that the presence of observers, even at a distance, may influence grazing activity (Jamieson and Hodgson, 1979b). Thus care should always be taken to minimise the amount of movement round plots. The use of an observation post which provides some shelter may be helpful, but animals often seem to be disturbed more by covert movements which they cannot locate than by more overt activities which they can readily identify. This is particularly true of night-time observations.

The majority of grazing activity occurs between dawn and dusk, but it is not safe to assume that no grazing will take place during the hours of darkness, even during the short nights of summer. Thus, truly comprehensive observation requires the provision of night-viewing facilities. A powerful flashlight or spotlight provides suitable illumination, and infra-red equipment and image-intensifiers have been used successfully for night studies.

It is a wise precaution to accustom animals to the night-viewing procedures of choice over periods of 1-2 hours for several nights preceding the start of a series of studies, but even then it is not necessarily safe to assume that there will be no interference with normal patterns of behaviour.

Several alternative data recording systems are available, ranging from simple notebooks through data recording forms and cards to portable dictaphones and data loggers. The use of data forms provides a structured format for controlling recording sequences and checking errors (Fig. 6.3), and mark-sense cards (IBM UK Ltd) eliminate the need for subsequent data punching. Small portable dictaphones have the advantage of flexibility, particularly for complex descriptive data, and data loggers are now becoming cheaper and more robust for field use. Most recording systems require the construction of a simple shorthand coding system. It is a wise precaution to make frequent notes of events like weather changes, or the movement of people or machinery, which might influence animal behaviour. Explanatory comments to amplify standardized recording procedures are also helpful.

Some preliminary experience of the normal pattern of grazing activity is essential. Where a team of observers is used it is important to organise preliminary training sessions and to take account of (and if possible eliminate) individual differences in recording efficiency. It is also helpful to deploy observers so as to minimise the risks of confounding observer differences with treatment and (where important) time-of-day effects.

Easy identification of animals in the field is important. Many alternative marking procedures have been used, ranging from painted numbers or stick-on coloured patches to coloured tassels. One of the most effective systems is the use of a cube or vertical prism with sides 8 x 8 cm mounted over the shoulders (G B Nicoll, personal communication). The fittings may be coloured or numbered on each face. Identification is more difficult in artificial light unless reflective paint is used.

6.4.1 Grazing time

It is possible to make virtually continuous records of the activity of small numbers of animals (eg Chambers, 1959), but manual recording of grazing time is almost invariably done on the basis of intermittent records in which animals are observed at intervals and a record made of their activity *at the time of observation* (section 6.2.1). Where ingestive behaviour is the sole interest, it will suffice to record "grazing" or "not grazing" at each observation. However, it would be usual to include observations on ruminating as well as grazing activity, and possibly also on the movements of animals, in most routine observations. Recording the extra information occupies little more time.

When observing a group or groups of animals, it is preferable to record activity for each animal individually rather than to categorise the numbers of animals engaged in particular activities. The former procedure ensures a better base for making statistical comparisons, and for relating behaviour to other variables (eg herbage intake) on an individual animal basis. However,

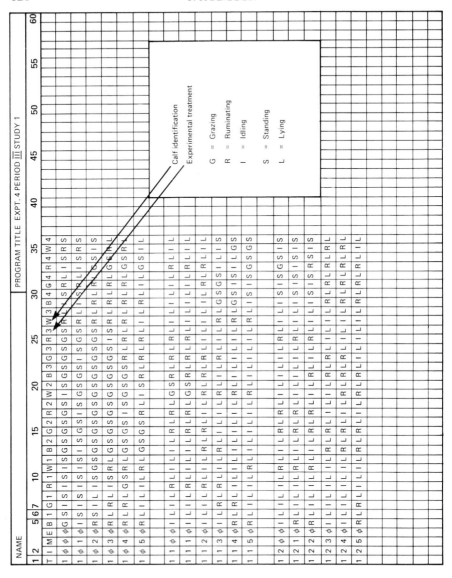

Fig. 6.3 Example of a data form used for recording field information on grazing and ruminating activity (from Jamieson, 1975)

it puts individual animal identification at a premium, and may limit the number of animals which can be recorded. It is important to make observations on groups and/or individuals in a regular sequence to avoid risks of missed or biased records, and for this purpose it is useful to make records directly onto a standard form on which the animals are identified individually (Fig. 6.3).

Using the procedures outlined above it would be reasonable for a single observer to make regular records on 20-30 animals at a time, split into several groups. A set of records of this size could be completed in about 5 min, depending upon the conditions and the complexity of the data. On a 10 min cycle this will allow a 5 min break from concentrated watching, or a short period in which to make other observations, of bite rate for example.

Manual systems allow records to be made on substantial numbers of animals at one time but because of the high labour demands the duration of observation is frequently limited to 24 hours. However, it is advisable to attempt records on at least two days (not necessarily consecutive) in a measurement period.

6.4.2 **Rate of biting**

It is important to determine in advance whether monitoring of biting rate is to be based on jaw movements or head movements. In practice, jaw movements will be difficult to observe accurately except at very close quarters, whereas head movements can normally be observed easily from a considerable distance and often when the animal is partly obscured.

It is also vital to decide the basis for accepting a grazing record. This question was discussed in section 6.2.2.

Records of biting rate are frequently made in association with observations on grazing time and periodicity, in which case the balanced distribution of records throughout the day (section 6.3.3) presents no difficulty. In other cases it is advisable to check the normal pattern of grazing activity in advance. Although bite rates are normally expressed in terms of the number of bites per unit time (bites min^{-1} or sec^{-1}) it is usually easier to record manually the time required for an animal to take a pre-determined number of bites and then to transform the results. For recording purposes it is useful to have a stop watch with a "hold" button so that a record can be interrupted if an animal stops grazing temporarily.

Using the 20-bite technique, measurements of biting rate can be made at a rate of at least one per minute during active periods of grazing. Thus it may often be possible to combine bite rate measurements with more general direct observations on grazing activity, particularly when the sampling interval technique is used. Using these standard procedures, one observer should be able to record bite rates on up to 20-30 animals, but would require some assistance for the combined recording of grazing activity and biting rate.

6.4.3 Rate of intake and intake per bite

Two basic procedures have been used to estimate short-term rates of intake and intake per bite. Allden and Whittaker (1970) fitted animals with apparatus to collect faeces and urine and measured their gain in weight over grazing periods of one hour. Corrections were also made for insensible weight losses in other animals which were prevented from grazing. Other workers (eg Stobbs, 1973) measured the weight of extrusa collected from animals fistulated at the oesophagus which were allowed to graze for periods of up to one hour, but usually for only 20-30 min. In each case records were made of the time which the animals actually spent grazing, and the number of bites taken over this period, using the procedures outlined above.

The former procedure has been less widely used than the latter. It does not involve the use of surgically prepared animals, but is dependent upon the effective prevention of losses of faeces and urine and requires very accurate field weighing facilities. It is unlikely to be suitable for work with cattle.

Procedures for the use of animals fistulated at the oesophagus are described in detail in Chapter 3. For estimates of RI and IB it is important to ensure quantitative recovery of the herbage ingested, and for this purpose it is usually necessary to place a cylindrical foam rubber plug in the oesophagus just below the fistula (Table 6.6). Plugs should be approximately 5-6 cm in diameter x 5 cm long for adult cattle, and 3 cm diameter x 3 cm long for adult sheep. Each plug is threaded on a nylon cord with a button at the end to prevent swallowing, and the cord fastened round the animal's neck or attached to the collection bag for security. Plugs of this kind are not always completely effective (Table 6.6), and should be replaced after two or three collections because they tend to lose their resilience. It is advisable to check the recovery of ingested herbage in preliminary hand-feeding trials and to reject animals giving variable or low recoveries. Some animals will not graze normally when a plug is fitted, and in most cases the use of a throat plug elicits an increase in the rate of saliva secretion.

For both procedures it is essential to work with small numbers of animals at a time so that individuals can be closely supervised. Where manual techniques are used each animal must be watched by an observer to ensure that complete records of grazing time and bite numbers are collected, but even when animals are fitted with automatic recording devices it is important to ensure close supervision during grazing. For manual recording procedures the animals should graze relatively small paddocks (100-500 m^2) to help to ensure that biting activity is always visible.

Table 6.6   The recovery of ingested herbage at an oesophageal fistula in animals with or without a throat plug fitted (from Jamieson, 1975).

	Recovery	
	Mean	Standard Deviation
Expt. 1		
Without throat plug[+]	0.69	0.222
With throat plug[+]	0.97	0.074
Expt. 2		
With throat plug[ø]	0.98	0.068

[+]3 calves x 3 collections
[ø]4 calves x 6 collections (results for one calf with erratic recoveries omitted).

6.5 FILM RECORDS

Film recording techniques, including time lapse and cine photography and, more recently, video recording, are essentially extensions of visual techniques. They have been widely used in research on animal behaviour, for example in observations on animal distribution, movement and agonistic behaviour. At present they are of limited value for studies on ingestive behaviour, however, except as a means of providing detailed records of particular activity patterns on either a macro or a micro scale. Still photographs do not provide a reliable basis for determining whether or not animals are ingesting herbage, and cine or video films of groups of animals can seldom be made with sufficient resolution to allow determination of bite rates.

These techniques are likely to be of particular value where the presence of observers would disturb animals unduly, for special applications like the use of infra-red cameras at night, and for circumstances where the comforts of indoor viewing outweigh the disadvantages of limited accuracy of interpretation. In many circumstances it would be advisable to consider the merits of alternative automatic recording procedures.

6.6 AUTOMATIC RECORDING OF GRAZING ACTIVITY

Continuous observation of animals on a 24 hour basis is laborious and time-consuming, and it is not surprising that many alternative procedures for the automatic recording of behaviour have been developed. In addition, automatic devices make it possible to record some activities (eg jaw movements) which would be virtually impossible to observe by eye in the field and to make detailed analyses of behaviour patterns. A comprehensive catalogue of devices available for recording grazing behaviour would occupy a book to itself, and the objective here is simply to consider the use and the limitations of some alternative devices in order to illustrate the range of options available. For further information and discussion of the principles involved readers are referred to textbooks by Mackay (1968), Zucker (1969), Fryer *et al* (1976), Klewe and Kimmich (1978) and Amlaner and MacDonald (1980).

There are essentially three phases in the automatic recording of grazing activity: sensing the activity of interest, and then transmitting and recording information from the sensors. For the purposes of this discussion it is convenient to consider behaviour sensing separate from the other two phases, though in practical systems the three phases are clearly inter-dependent. In many cases the data transmission and recording phases are in effect combined. Data processing procedures will not be considered, though automatic data collection systems obviously lend themselves to automatic data processing and may also allow some preliminary condensing of information in the recording phase.

Most automatic systems involve the mounting of sensors on the head of the animal, and recording or transmitting equipment on the head or shoulders, using harnesses developed for the purpose. The maximum weight of equipment to be carried should be of the order of 1 kg for sheep and 10 kg for cattle, but with present-day miniaturised equipment these physical limits are unlikely to be approached. It may be more difficult to ensure that the harnesses and fittings do not themselves interfere with the animals' natural movements.

Recording of grazing activity is based on the use of devices to sense movement of either the jaw or the head of the animal, usually coupled with an assessment of whether or not the head and neck are held below the horizontal (and therefore, presumably, in a grazing position). This approach may allow the recording of both grazing (head down) and ruminating (head up) jaw activity.

Jaw or head movements may be sensed and recorded in the form of a continuously variable (analogue) trace in which the output from the sensor bears some relationship to the magnitude of the movement concerned (Fig. 6.5). Analogue records allow detailed analysis of the form and pattern of particular movements but they are unnecessarily complex for most purposes, and require a separate analysis phase. A simpler alternative is to record each movement as it occurs on an "event recorder" or digital counter, which can then be used to summarise activity as a rate (number per unit time) or a cumulative total over time. For this purpose sensor output need have no quantitative relationship to the movement in question so long as it is adequate to trigger the counter, but in many systems simple counters are set to respond to analogue signals of specified amplitude.

In all automatic systems decisions have to be made about the amplitude and frequency of signals which can be accepted as indicative of grazing activity, either in relation to the initial setting of sensing and recording devices or in the ultimate analysis of records. These decisions are essentially the same as those which have to be made in manual recording procedures, though in automatic systems they may be made more objectively and with greater consistency. Whatever the equipment used, it is essential to evaluate the records against appropriate visual checks. Signal output is likely to vary both between and within animals, depending upon the positioning, security and sensitivity of individual sensors, so it is important to calibrate equipment regularly.

Mechanical and pneumatic devices for recording ingestive behaviour are considered briefly in section 6.6.1, and electronic devices in section 6.6.2.

6.6.1 Mechanical and pneumatic devices

Probably the most widely used piece of equipment in grazing behaviour studies is the Kienzle Vibracorder (Kienzle Apparate GmbH, D-7730 Villingen, W Germany. UK agents: Lucas Kienzle Instruments, 36 Gravelly Industrial Park, Birmingham, B24 8TA). This equipment uses a vibrating pendulum, the movement of which is recorded by a stylus onto a circular disc driven by a clockwork motor. The pendulum responds to movements of the animal's head or body, but the unit is mounted in such a way that it is only activated when the animal is in the head-down (and presumed grazing) position. Head movements with the muzzle close to the ground can occur in the absence of grazing, but in practice they are uncommon. The Vibracorder was originally used for sheep, and gave satisfactory results when mounted on a harness on the animal's shoulder (Allden, 1962). This is still the position of choice for sheep. For cattle, vibracorders have been fitted on the neck (Stobbs, 1970) or suspended under the chin, but the most satisfactory performance appears to be obtained when the unit is mounted on the animal's cheek, using a base-plate fixed to a head-stall and neck-strap. Recording periods ranging from 12 hours to 8 days are available on different models.

The Vibracorder has been widely used to record grazing time and periodicity. The trace is seldom sharp enough to identify individual head movements, however (Fig. 6.4), even in the version giving one chart revolution every 3 h, so it cannot realistically be used to record the number of bites or biting rate. Jones and Cowper (1975) found that the vibracorder over-estimated grazing time by 18.3% compared with visual observations though Jamieson (1975) found a virtually 1:1 relationship over a series of swards between vibracorder estimates and visual observations at 10 min intervals.

The instrument has the advantages of robustness and simplicity though, because it is sited in a vulnerable position on the animal, it is advisable to protect it from accidental damage. Water ingress can also be a problem; the use of a 10cm section cut from a car inner tube has proved to be a reasonably effective preventative, and also provides some physical protection to the instrument.

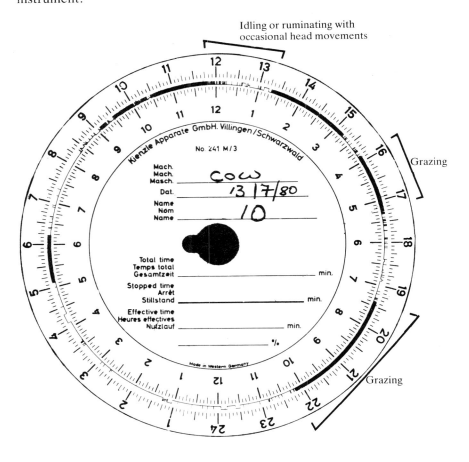

Fig. 6.4   Example of a vibracorder trace, showing a sequence of periods of grazing activity over 24 hours (from Jamieson, 1975)

Regular maintenance of the motor and pendulum, and careful placing of the unit on the animal, are essential for the production of clear traces. Even then a degree of subjectivity is often required in interpretation, particularly during periods of intermittent and desultory grazing or of fly interference. Preliminary training in the use of the equipment (for both animals and staff) is essential, and should include comparative studies with visual observations over varying periods of time. It is unrealistic to expect to read the version giving one chart revolution in 24 hours to a resolution much better than 5 minute intervals.

Pneumatic devices, normally incorporating a balloon fitted inside a strap under the jaw or over the *masseter* muscle, have been used to monitor chewing activity for many years (eg Balch, 1958). The device itself is effective and reliable so long as it is carefully placed, but it has seldom been used on free-grazing animals because of the unwieldliness of most of the associated recording equipment. A variant of the Vibracorder system, in which the stylus is driven by a pneumatic plunger, has been developed by Bechet (1978) and is claimed to allow the recording of individual jaw movements.

6.6.2 **Electrical and electronic devices**

Electrical and electronic devices have been used to respond to variation in head position, head movement, jaw movement, or some combination of the three. Other procedures are theoretically possible, for example monitoring the proximity of the mouth to the sward, or the movement of food and digesta down and up the oesophagus, but so far they have not been used extensively in grazing studies.

The output from appropriate sensors may be recorded as a continuous trace or analogue signal for subsequent analysis, or summarised as a running total of events or binary counts on an event recorder. Information is commonly collected and stored in multi-channel recorders, allowing the simultaneous recording of several items of information from one animal or of simpler information from several animals at once, thus providing great flexibility in animal monitoring.

Information may be recorded in the form of a paper trace or tape recording, or in electronic counters. It is usually simpler and cheaper to record and store information on the animal for later collection. This allows continuous recording of information from each animal, but requires one recorder per animal, and monitoring of the effectiveness of individual recorders can be difficult unless a visual indicator is fitted to each. A single master recorder can be used to service several individual sensing systems by means of radio-telemetry, but this usually necessitates the use of a sampling sequence, and multiple recording systems of this kind can be expensive. In this case care will be needed to ensure that sampling periods are long enough to identify current activity and, where necessary, activity rates correctly. Hybrid systems are available in which information is recorded continuously on animal-mounted recorders which are interrogated at intervals from a remote station.

Systems for recording physiological parameters are available commercially, as are radio-telemetry systems for field use. However, the success rate for "off the peg" systems in grazing work is not good. For anyone contemplating the use of telemetry systems it is advisable to keep the equipment as simple as possible, to ensure that it is tailored to meet the requirements of a particular project, and to ensure that expert help is available to maintain the equipment.

6.6.2.1 *Position of the head.* It is assumed that when the animal is standing with its muzzle close to the ground it is likely to be grazing. Animals may adopt this posture without grazing, and may graze when lying down, so both positive and negative errors are possible. However, they are unlikely to be important, except perhaps in particularly hot weather or when flies are a nuisance, and even then positive errors can be minimised if records of head position and jaw or head movement are linked.

A convenient sensor is the mercury switch (Jones and Cowper, 1975) in which contact between two adjacent electrodes is made or broken by movement of mercury in a canal whose alignment to the horizontal can be adjusted to allow a sensitive assessment of head or neck alignment. The mercury switch can be mounted on the neck or shoulder of the animal, or on the head. Alternatively, the position of the head can be monitored using a switch responding to the tension in an elastic cord running between harnesses on head and shoulders. This is a relatively simple device, though the tensioning of the cord and setting of the switch can be difficult and the cord itself is susceptible to interference from other animals. Devices of this kind are normally used in association with jaw movement sensors in the dual evaluation of grazing and ruminating activity.

Both the mercury switch and the neck cord can provide a reliable indication of head position when set correctly, but they are likely to need careful adjustment to suit individual animals and particular sward conditions. They may be useless as indicators of grazing activity on tall swards and sloping terrain.

6.6.2.2 *Jaw movements.* The commonest form of jaw movement record involves the use of a switch responding to changes in tension in a cord looped underneath the jaw (Chambers *et al*, 1981), but several alternative switch designs are in use (eg Stobbs and Cowper, 1972). The adjustment of switch setting may be critical for reliable recording. Recent innovations include the use of a carbon-packed tube (P D Penning, personal communication) and a variable inductance gauge (Leveille *et al*, 1979) to sense jaw movements. For all of these devices the animal simply has to be trained to wear a head stall and fittings. Other devices which have been used in indoor studies include electrodes to record tooth contact, either fitted to teeth or implanted in them (Kydd and Mullins, 1963), and electrodes placed over (Nichols, 1966) or implanted over the *masseter* muscle to monitor the electromyogram. These alternatives have not been adopted for grazing studies, probably because of the degree of interference with the animal.

All jaw movement recorders require a means of distinguishing between eating and ruminating activity. This is relatively simple where a continuous analogue record is made, because ruminating jaw movements are characteristically much more uniform in frequency and amplitude than are grazing movements (Fig. 6.5). When jaw movements are simply counted as events it is necessary to monitor head position at the same time, so that jaw movements in the "head down" position are recorded as grazing, and those associated with the "head up" position are recorded as ruminating. In practice it may be easier to record total jaw movement and grazing movements on separate channels of information, ruminating movements being estimated by difference.

It is possible to record the degree of jaw movement quantitatively as an analogue signal if an appropriate sensor is used (Chambers *et al*, 1981, Fig 6.5) but this is seldom attempted in the field.

6.6.2.3 *Head movements.* Though head movements have been used as a routine indication of grazing activity in manual studies for many years, and more recently as the basis for Vibracorder records, they have not been used in electronic recording systems until recently, when Chambers *et al* (1981) used an accelerometer to monitor grazing activity (Fig 6.5). This provides an alternative method of differentiating between grazing and ruminating activity, since the latter is unlikely to be associated with the vigorous acceleration movements which characterise the former. However, it is still advisable to use a "head down" restriction in order to screen out other random head movements. Head accelerations are better defined in sheep than in cattle, and vary in different sward conditions, so discriminating circuits are likely to need adjustment for different animal species and different swards.

6.7 CONCLUSIONS

This has been of necessity a somewhat cursory treatment of a subject which is still rapidly evolving. Readers should investigate thoroughly the

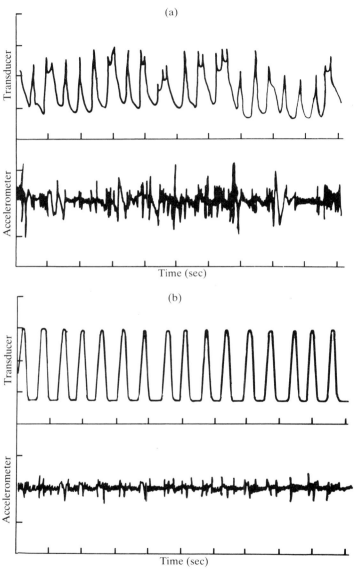

Fig. 6.5 *Oscilloscope traces of the output from a displacement transducer recording jaw movements (upper) and an accelerometer recording head movements (lower) in a sheep during periods of (a) grazing and (b) ruminating. Horizontal scale 1 sec per division; vertical scales 0.5 cm per division (upper), 5 m/sec² per division (lower) (from Chambers et al, 1981)*

available procedures and items of equipment, with the aid of an experienced adviser if possible, before deciding upon the alternatives which suit their requirements best. Modern electronic techniques make it possible to monitor patterns of behaviour in great detail, but informed decisions about the important parameters to measure, and how to measure them, depend ultimately upon the experience gained by watching animals in the field. Readers contemplating the use of automatic equipment should consider the possible influence of the equipment itself upon the behaviour patterns of interest, and should remember they may still be required to make subjective judgements on the significance of the patterns observed. Finally, it is important to emphasise that the subject itself is very much in a stage of development, as exemplified by the lack of definition of several of the parameters discussed in this chapter. It is often difficult to divorce the results of measurements on aspects of ingestive behaviour from the procedures used to obtain them, and this should be borne in mind both in deciding upon a measurement routine and in making comparisons between sets of observations obtained in different ways.

6.8 REFERENCES

ALLDEN, W G (1962). Rate of herbage intake and grazing time in relation to herbage availability. *Proceedings of the Australian Society of Animal Production*, 4, 163-166.

ALLDEN, W G and WHITTAKER, I A McD (1970). The determinants of herbage intake by grazing sheep: the interrelationship of factors influencing herbage intake and availability. *Australian Journal of Agricultural Research*, 21, 755-766.

AMLANER, C J and MacDONALD, D W (1980) (eds.) A Handbook on Biotelemetry and Radio Tracking. *Proceedings of an International Conference on Telemetry and Radio Tracking in Biology and Medicine*, Oxford, 1979. Oxford: Pergammon Press, 804 pp.

ARNOLD, G W (1981). Grazing behaviour. In: F.H.W. Morley (ed). *World Animal Science, B.1. Grazing Animals* Amsterdam: Elsevier pp 79-104.

ARNOLD, G W and DUDZINSKI, M L (1978). *Developments in Animal and Veterinary Sciences, 2. Ethology of Free-Ranging Domestic Animals* Amsterdam: Elsevier, 198 pp.

BALCH, C C (1958). Observations on the act of eating in cattle. *British Journal of Nutrition*, 12, 330-345.

BÉCHET, G (1978). Enregistrement des activités alimentaires et meryciques des ovins au pâturage. *Annales de Zootechnie*, 27, 107-113.

CHACON, E, STOBBS, T H and SANDLAND, R L (1976). Estimation of herbage consumption by grazing cattle using measurements of eating behaviour. *Journal of the British Grassland Society*, 31, 81-87.

CHAMBERS, A R M, HODGSON, J and MILNE, J A (1981). The development and use of equipment for the automatic recording of ingestive behaviour in sheep and cattle. *Grass and Forage Science*, 36, 97-105.

CHAMBERS, D T (1959). Grazing behaviour of calves reared at pasture. *Journal of Agricultural Science, Cambridge*, 53, 417-424.

COMBELLAS, J and HODGSON, J (1979). Herbage intake and milk production by grazing dairy cows. 1. The effects of variation in herbage mass and daily herbage allowance in a short-term trial. *Grass and Forage Science*, 34, 209-214.

FRYER, T B, MILLER, H A and SANDLER, H (1976) (eds). Biotelemetry III *Proceedings of the Third International Symposium on Biotelemetry*, California, 1976. London: Academic Press, 381 pp.

GARY, L A, SHERRIT, G W and HALE, E B (1970). Behaviour of Charolais cattle on pasture. *Journal of Animal Science*, 30, 203-206.

HAFEZ, E S E (1969) (ed). *The behaviour of domestic animals*. 2nd edn. London: Balliere, Tindall and Cox, 440 pp.

HANCOCK, J (1950). Studies on monozygotic cattle twins. IV. Uniformity trials: grazing behaviour. *New Zealand Journal of Science and Technology*, 32, 22-59.

HANCOCK, J (1953). Grazing behaviour of cattle. *Animal Breeding Abstracts* 21, 1-13.

JAMIESON, W S (1975). *Studies on the herbage intake and grazing behaviour of cattle and sheep.* Ph.D. thesis, University of Reading, 187 pp.

JAMIESON, W S and HODGSON, J (1979a). The effect of daily herbage allowance and sward characteristics upon the ingestive behaviour and herbage intake of calves under strip-grazing management. *Grass and Forage Science*, 34, 261-271.

JAMIESON, W S and HODGSON, J (1979b). The effects of variation in sward characteristics upon the ingestive behaviour and herbage intake of calves and lambs under a continuous stocking management. *Grass and Forage Science*, 34, 273-282.

JONES, R J and COWPER, L J (1975). A lightweight electronic device for measurement of grazing time of cattle. *Tropical Grasslands*, 9, 235-241.

KLEWE, H J and KIMMICH, H P (1978) (eds). Biotelemetry IV. *Proceedings of the Fourth International Symposium on Biotelemetry*, Germany, 1978. Braunschweig: Döring, 277 pp.

KYDD, W L and MULLINS, G (1963). A telemetry system for intraoral pressures. *Archives of Oral Biology*, 8, 235-236.

LE DU, Y L P, COMBELLAS, J, HODGSON, J and BAKER, R D (1979). Herbage intake and milk production by grazing dairy cows. 2. The effects of level of winter feeding and daily herbage allowance. *Grass and Forage Science*, 34, 249-260.

LEVEILLE, M, JOUANY, J P and BRUN, J P (1979). Analyse automatique du compartement alimentaire et merycique chez le mouton. *Annales de Biologie Animale Biochimie, Biophysique*, 19, 889-893.

MACKAY, R S (1968). *Bio-Medical Telemetry: Sensing and Transmitting Biological Information from Animals and Man.* London: John Wiley and Sons, 388 pp.

NICHOLS, G DE LA M (1966). Radio transmission of sheep's jaw movements. *New Zealand Journal of Agricultural Research*, 9, 468-473.

RODRIGUEZ CAPRILES, J M (1973). *The herbage intake of young grazing cattle.* Ph.D. thesis, University of Reading, 177 pp.

SNEDECOR, G W and COCHRAN, W G (1967). *Statistical Methods.* 6th end. Ames: Iowa State University Press, 593 pp.

SPEDDING, C R W, LARGE, R V and KYDD, D D (1966). The evaluation of herbage species by grazing animals. *Proceedings of the 10th International Grassland Congress, Helsinki*, pp 479-483.

STOBBS, T H (1970). Automatic measurement of grazing time by dairy cows on tropical grass and legume pastures. *Tropical Grasslands*, 4, 237-244.

STOBBS, T H (1973). The effect of plant structure on the intake of tropical pastures. I. Variation in the bite size of grazing cattle. *Australian Journal of Agricultural Research*, 24, 809-819.

STOBBS, T H and COWPER, L J (1972). Automatic measurement of the jaw movements of dairy cows during grazing and rumination. *Tropical Grasslands*, 6, 67-69.

ZUCKER, M H (1969). *Electronic circuits for behavioural and biometrical sciences.* A reference book of useful solid-state circuits. San Francisco: W.H. Freeman and Co. 241 pp.

INDEX

PRINTED BY INPRINT OF LUTON (Designers & Printers) LTD.